PLAYING WITH PURPOSE

TACKLING TRUTH

MIKE YORKEY

PLAYING WITH PURPOSE

TACKLING TRUTH

Spiritual Insights Drawn from the
Great Game of Football

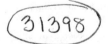

BARBOUR BOOKS

An Imprint of Barbour Publishing, Inc.

Published by Barbour Books, an imprint of Barbour Publishing, Inc., P.O. Box 719, Uhrichsville, Ohio 44683, www.barbourbooks.com.

Our mission is to publish and distribute inspirational products offering exceptional value and biblical encouragement to the masses.

ecpa Member of the
Evangelical Christian
Publishers Association

Printed in the United States of America.

Welcome to
Playing with Purpose:
TACKLING TRUTH

Is it appropriate to combine America's favorite sport with God's Word? Of course!

The apostle Paul wrote the sports of his day into letters that became our scriptures. You'll find biblical lessons related to running races (1 Corinthians 9:24), wrestling (Ephesians 6:12), even boxing (1 Corinthians 9:26). So why shouldn't we draw insights from the great game of football?

In the pages ahead, you'll find devotional readings that highlight some intriguing aspect of big-time football—either major college or NFL—each coupled with a brief, thought-provoking spiritual point. Read the stories for love of the game; mull the takeaways for love of the Lord.

After every fifteenth devotional, you will find a profile of a Christian player of recent years, drawn from Barbour Publishing's Playing with Purpose series. Those books were written by Mike Yorkey, who serves as editor of this devotional, and provide an in-depth view of the careers and spiritual journeys of several intriguing players, coaches, and other individuals connected to the game we love.

Within these pages you'll find spiritual truths to inform, encourage, and challenge you as you live your own Christian life each day.

PAUL KENT, GLENN HASCALL, LEE WARREN, ALLEN PALMERI, TRACY SUMNER, JOSH COOLEY, AND RUSSELL WIGHT, WRITERS

MIKE YORKEY, SERIES EDITOR

I AM SECOND

He doesn't have the same notoriety as the quarterbacks he filled in for—Johnny Unitas and Bob Griese—but when Earl Morrall died in 2014, he was recognized as one of the NFL's best-ever backups.

A product of Michigan State University, where he won a Rose Bowl and played in the College World Series, Morrall was the second pick of the 1956 draft, by San Francisco. Traded to Pittsburgh the next year, he became a starter, making the Pro Bowl after a 6–6 season. But Morrall earned greater fame more than a decade later, replacing injured signal callers on three Super Bowl teams.

With Baltimore in 1968, Morrall took the helm when superstar Unitas went down in the preseason. Morrall led the Colts to a 13–1 record and Super Bowl appearance against the Jets, winning the league MVP award. Two years later, still with the Colts, Morrall replaced an injured Unitas *in* the Super Bowl, directing a come-from-behind victory over Dallas.

In 1972, as a thirty-eight-year-old with Miami, Morrall was tapped again when Bob Griese broke a leg in Week 5. The backup-turned-starter continued Griese's winning ways, leading the Dolphins to nine straight victories in a 14–0 regular season, plus a 20–14 win over Cleveland in the AFC divisional playoff. Griese returned partway through the AFC championship game with Pittsburgh, then started the Super Bowl against Washington. A 14–7 victory completed the NFL's only perfect season.

Through it all, Morrall just served when needed—and won. "I've always said Unitas, Griese, and Dan Marino are in the Hall of Fame," said Dolphins coach Don Shula. "Earl is in my own personal hall of fame."

That's generally how others feel about the person who lives the truth of Philippians 2:3: "Do nothing out of selfish ambition or vain conceit. Rather, in humility value others above yourselves."

Humble yourselves before the Lord, and he will lift you up.
JAMES 4:10

FREE INDEED

It's no surprise that the player who holds the record for most interceptions in NFL history is a free safety. Paul Krause played the position at a Hall of Fame level for the Washington Redskins and Minnesota Vikings.

In a standard defense, a free safety is free to go to the ball. On a pass play he typically locates the deepest receiver. If the ball is thrown elsewhere, he is free to read the quarterback's eyes and move accordingly. If he does his job well, as Krause did for so many years, interceptions will come. Using his freedom for good, Krause snagged 81 interceptions from 1964 to 1979.

Krause displayed an impressive consistency throughout his long NFL career. He was steady and sure, with a self-described "even-keel intensity." Krause always knew what he could and could not do, and he did very well.

Christians—who have God's Holy Spirit inside—are free to live well. Our human nature, what some Bible translations call "the flesh," may interfere, but it need not derail us. In fact, we are taught to not let our spiritual liberty become an opportunity for the flesh: "You, my brothers and sisters, were called to be free. But do not use your freedom to indulge the flesh; rather, serve one another humbly in love" (Galatians 5:13). With discipline this can become a habit. And the head is certainly involved.

"I think I was a student of the game in my own respect," Krause once said. "I knew what the offense was trying to do to the defense. I believe I knew that if the offense was doing certain things, I knew what the other twenty-one guys on the field should be doing."

You'll probably never be a Hall of Fame free safety. But in Christ, you are certainly free to live well.

"So if the Son sets you free, you will be free indeed."
JOHN 8:36

A NEW HOPE

Rex Ryan didn't waste any time.

On February 24, 2011—with Green Bay's Super Bowl XLV victory over Pittsburgh barely three weeks old—the New York Jets head coach issued a bold declaration at the NFL Scouting Combine.

"I believe this is the year we're going to win the Super Bowl," Ryan proclaimed. "The fact is when I thought we'd win it the first two years, I *guarantee* we'll win it this year."

Ryan, as it turns out, should probably ditch the prophecy business and stick with X's and O's. The Jets finished 8–8 that season.

To be fair, Ryan isn't the only one making such outrageous claims. In 2013, Atlanta wide receiver Roddy White said the upcoming season was "Super Bowl or bust" before the Falcons went 4–12. That same year, Washington head coach Mike Shanahan said his players "have set the expectations. Anything short of a Super Bowl is a failure." The Redskins went 3–13.

For each team, every off-season brings new hope—no matter how far-fetched. February to August is the NFL's period of renewal, when all thirty-two teams dream of winning a Lombardi Trophy the following year.

But Christians have a new hope that's not far-fetched at all. Every believer, as 1 Peter 1:3 says, has a "living hope" through the "new birth" that comes from Jesus. This new birth is what Jesus describes in John 3:3 as being "born again." It's the moment when God renews our sinful hearts and generously gives us spiritual life through faith in Jesus. This living hope assures us that we are forgiven through Christ, made right with a holy God, and guaranteed to enter His eternal kingdom.

That is true hope!

Praise be to the God and Father of our Lord Jesus Christ!
In his great mercy he has given us new birth into a living hope
through the resurrection of Jesus Christ from the dead.
1 PETER 1:3

UNTOUCHABLE, UNSTOPPABLE. . .AND REMEMBERED

In a sixteen-year NFL career, Marcus Allen caught nearly 600 passes for more than 5,400 yards, and rushed more than 3,000 times for over 12,000 yards. He was a six-time Pro Bowl selection and won the AP Offensive Rookie of the Year, Most Valuable Player, Offensive Player of the Year, and Comeback Player of the Year awards. He was a member of the Oakland Raiders when they won Super Bowl XVIII in 1984, earning the game MVP trophy.

In recalling the 38–9 victory over the Washington Redskins, Allen said, "I was really untouchable, unstoppable that game. But it was heightened on one particular play, and that was the longest run where everything completely slowed down." Specifically, Allen was describing a third-quarter play in which he ran one direction only to be met by a wall of defenders, then reversed course looking for a hole. At midfield Allen burst through the line for a 74-yard touchdown run, the longest in Super Bowl history at the time.

Few who watched that game on television will recall the advertisements. What they'll remember is a player—now a Hall of Famer—with an uncanny instinct and follow-through. As Allen says of his performance that day, "My awareness was so keen, it was so heightened, it was really amazing."

Few of us have ever played professional football—but we know skill and dedication when we see it. Deep down, don't you want the same dedication in your own life toward the things you really care about? As the apostle Paul once wrote, "Whether you eat or drink or whatever you do, do it all for the glory of God" (1 Corinthians 10:31).

> *Whatever you do, work at it with all your heart, as working for the Lord, not for human masters, since you know that you will receive an inheritance from the Lord as a reward. It is the Lord Christ you are serving.*
> COLOSSIANS 3:23–24

PATIENCE...

Twenty-six years between Super Bowl wins might seem petty for fans of NFL teams who have waited longer (or are still waiting for that first title)—but for Pittsburgh backers, it felt like an eternity between the Steelers' fourth championship in 1980 and fifth in 2006.

After the Steelers won their fourth Super Bowl in six years, defensive tackle "Mean Joe" Greene coined the phrase "one for the thumb in '81." Greene was thirty-four when he made that statement. . .and he retired after that '81 season with a bare thumb. Teammate Lynn Swann quit after the next season, and Terry Bradshaw followed suit in '83. Heading into the '84 season, Franco Harris moved on to Seattle.

As personnel changed, the Steelers entered a long championship drought, including a stretch from 1985 to '91 in which they made the playoffs just once. The team eventually returned to its winning ways, reaching the Super Bowl in 1996—though they lost that game to the Cowboys. Then, in early 2006, second-year quarterback Ben Roethlisberger finally led the team to its fifth title with a 21–10 Super Bowl victory over Seattle. They also won in 2009 with Big Ben at the helm.

Championships do not necessarily define success, but they certainly are the goal. Players and fans alike must be patient as teams pursue talent and develop it into championship material.

For Christians, heaven is the ultimate goal. But while we're still on earth, we need patience with ourselves and others as the Holy Spirit shapes us into Jesus' image. As the apostle Paul told Christians in Philippi, "Being confident of this, that he who began a good work in you will carry it on to completion until the day of Christ Jesus" (Philippians 1:6).

May your whole spirit, soul and body be kept
blameless at the coming of our Lord Jesus Christ.
The one who calls you is faithful, and he will do it.
1 THESSALONIANS 5:23–24

NO WORK, ALL GRACE

From the moment a team hoists the Lombardi Trophy in early February, the clock starts ticking on the new NFL season. The road to a Super Bowl championship is an arduous twelve-month grind that is literally filled with blood, sweat, and—yes—even some tears. Three hundred-pound offensive linemen have emotions, too.

Things get rolling in late February with the scouting combine. After that, it's a hodgepodge of voluntary minicamps, the draft, rookie minicamps, mandatory minicamps, organized team activities, training camps, and preseason games—all leading up to the regular-season kickoff in early September. From there, it's four drama-filled months just to determine who reaches the playoffs.

Phew.

Any serious Super Bowl contender must put in an extraordinary amount of effort and hard work to achieve glory. Christians, on the other hand, do not. Scripture is quite clear that salvation comes only by God's grace through faith. Consider the following passages:

"He has saved us and called us to a holy life—not because of anything we have done but because of his own purpose and grace" (2 Timothy 1:9).

"He saved us, not because of righteous things we had done, but because of his mercy" (Titus 3:5).

"For it is by grace you have been saved, through faith—and this is not from yourselves, it is the gift of God—not by works, so that no one can boast" (Ephesians 2:8–9).

We can't impress God or earn forgiveness through human achievement. Salvation is a marvelous gift of His love. All we have to do is trust in the Savior who made it possible—Jesus Christ.

God's Son did all the hard work for us. Be thankful!

"A person is not justified by the works
of the law, but by faith in Jesus Christ."
GALATIANS 2:16

SECOND CHANCES

In his first five years as an NFL head coach, his team had one winning season and an overall record of 36–44. By the next season, the Cleveland Browns had moved to Baltimore and become the Ravens without Bill Belichick. He was potentially finished as a head coach.

Five years later, Belichick gained a second chance when Robert Kraft hired him to lead the New England Patriots. He quickly proved himself. From 2003 to 2012, Belichick's Patriots won 126 regular-season games and 140 games total, the most by any team over a ten-year period. Included in that span were a twenty-one-game winning streak and three Super Bowl championships. At the beginning of the 2014 season, NFL.com ranked Bill Belichick as the top head coach in the league. The second chance Robert Kraft offered had paid off handsomely.

You'll find second chances in the Bible, too. One begins in Acts 13, as Paul and Barnabas, on a journey to preach the Gospel, saw young John Mark desert the mission.

Some time later, as Paul and Barnabas prepared for another missionary trip, Barnabas suggested bringing along John. Paul disagreed with Barnabas, and their division was so strong that the two missionaries went their separate ways.

But fast-forward a few years. Paul, nearing the end of his life, writes a letter to his protégé Timothy. At this point, Paul had only Luke with him, and wanted more helpers for his ministry in Rome. So Paul urged Timothy to "come to me quickly," but also offered a second chance to the man who had once walked away. "Get Mark and bring him with you," Paul wrote, "because he is helpful to me in my ministry" (2 Timothy 4:9, 11).

Would you be willing to give someone a second chance? Would you be willing to accept a second chance?

You then, my son, be strong in the grace that is in Christ Jesus.
2 TIMOTHY 2:1

KNOW THE SIGNALS

Though NFL referees have been fitted with wireless microphones for all preseason, regular-season, and playoff games since 1975, they also communicate visually through a clearly defined type of "sign language."

Even the most casual fan of the game recognizes the both-arms-upraised signal for a field goal, touchdown, or successful point-after-touchdown attempt. When a referee rotates his forearms, he's indicating a false start by the offense. A circling of the entire arm means "time in," a signal to restart the game clock after a break.

What if the referee touches his right hand to the top of his cap? (Ineligible receiver. . .or an ineligible member of the kicking team downfield.) Or what if the ref puts both hands behind his head—looking a bit like he's ready to lie down for a nap? (Loss of down.)

Those are among thirty-six official signals, which, with minor variations, can communicate nearly four dozen aspects of the game relating to scoring, rule violations, and timing. Football officials standardized the signals and committed them to the rule book to keep everyone—officials, players, and fans alike—"on the same page."

God did much the same thing with His Word. Though He used around thirty-six writers, over some sixteen hundred years, He made sure the message was consistent and clear, carried through the years for the benefit of all who would believe its good news about Jesus Christ. As one of those writers, the apostle Paul said it, "All Scripture is God-breathed and is useful for teaching, rebuking, correcting and training in righteousness, so that the servant of God may be thoroughly equipped for every good work" (2 Timothy 3:16–17).

Are you as familiar with your Bible as you are a football referee's signals?

Consult God's instruction and the testimony of warning. If anyone does not speak according to this word, they have no light of dawn.
ISAIAH 8:20

HEART TO WIN

New England's Tom Brady has put together one of the top careers in NFL quarterback history, with four Super Bowl championships and two NFL MVP awards entering the 2016 season.

What makes Brady's work so intriguing is his total lack of fanfare entering the league. He is notorious for being one of the least impressive prospects in the NFL Combine, with a "speed" of 5.28 seconds in the 40-yard dash. Brady also had an ordinary physique and a seemingly average arm. The Patriots took him in the sixth round of the 2000 draft, the 199th player overall.

But Brady had those "intangibles" you often hear mentioned. Given the opportunity to play, he proved he could perform on the biggest stage, leading his Patriots to a 20–17 victory over St. Louis in Super Bowl XXXVI. At the time, Brady was the youngest quarterback to win the big game.

What made Brady so good at a level where many assumed he would fail?

His attributes have now been widely chronicled. He has heart, passion, and intelligence. He may not throw the fastest pass, but it's generally accurate. His high school teammates from San Mateo, California, say that Brady's work ethic and humility remain intact. And then there's that determination that kept him trying when he fell to No. 7 on the Michigan Wolverines' quarterback depth chart.

Many Bible heroes also overcame weaknesses to accomplish amazing things. For example, Gideon thought he was the weakest person in his own insignificant family, but God's angel called him a "mighty warrior" (Judges 6:12). King David asked, "Who am I, Sovereign Lord, and what is my family, that you have brought me this far?" (2 Samuel 7:18).

What's the common element? God—and a man's willingness to let God work through him.

The Sovereign Lord is my strength; he makes my feet like the feet of a deer, he enables me to tread on the heights.
Habakkuk 3:19

THE LOSING STREAK

The biggest way an NFL team misses the mark is by failing to win. A problem like that that continues for two seasons is a sporting sin of biblical proportions.

From September 12, 1976, to December 4, 1977, the Tampa Bay Buccaneers lost *twenty-six* consecutive games. That stretch set the standard for the longest losing streak in North American major professional sports, one that has since been tied by two NBA teams, the Cleveland Cavaliers and the Philadelphia 76ers.

The Bucs were an expansion team. At one point Coach John McKay was asked about his team's execution. "I'm in favor of it," he said.

It was no joking matter when the scribes and Pharisees brought a woman to Jesus. She had been caught in adultery, and the religious leaders wanted her to be executed by stoning. Jesus, though, put her failure in its proper perspective—which is that every last one of us needs to be rescued from sin. He would not define the woman by her adultery. "Go now and leave your life of sin," Jesus said. (See the whole story in John 8:1–11.)

Neither were the Tampa Bay Buccaneers ultimately defined by their fault-ridden start. They ended their losing streak by defeating the New Orleans Saints in Game 13 of their second season. And after the 2002 season, they accomplished something that several other NFL franchises have yet to do—win a Super Bowl.

There's a parallel here for Christians. We are all caught in the losing streak of sin. . .but we can find both the first victory (salvation) and the ultimate win (heaven) through Jesus Christ and God's Holy Spirit. And none of that takes work on our part. If we simply believe, it's all a gift of God's grace.

For sin shall no longer be your master,
because you are not under the law, but under grace.
ROMANS 6:14

IMPERFECT INTENTIONS

He'd only missed two extra point attempts all season. His field goal percentage was around 65 percent. His 115 points had led the Miami Dolphins to a perfect 14–0 season. Now, Garo Yepremian positioned himself to kick a 42-yard field goal to put Super Bowl VII out of reach of the Washington Redskins. A successful kick could result in a 17–0 shutout and a flawless 17–0 season.

What actually happened stunned Dolphin fans. Yepremian approached the snapped ball and sent it on its course, but Redskin defender Bill Brundige broke through to block the kick. As the football bounded back toward Yepremian, he made a split-second decision not to fall on the ball but to attempt a pass. If successful, the Dolphins might have held the shutout or even extended their lead—but the good intentions of the kicker resulted in an interception by Mike Bass, who scampered through an empty backfield to score Washington's only touchdown. Final score: 14–7.

The perfect season remained intact for the Dolphins, but the botched play in the Super Bowl still competes for attention. When Garo Yepremian retired in 1981, he had 210 successful field goal attempts—but the one he is most remembered for is the one he'd like to forget.

The past can play with our minds, reminding us of failure, making us think we are incapable of anything better than our most imperfect moments. Attitudes like that can keep us from even attempting something more, but the apostle Paul urged Christians to leave the past in the past: "One thing I do: Forgetting what is behind and straining toward what is ahead, I press on toward the goal to win the prize for which God has called me heavenward in Christ Jesus" (Philippians 3:13–14).

Sounds like Paul could identify with Garo Yepremian. Perhaps you can, too?

Do not conform to the pattern of this world,
but be transformed by the renewing of your mind.
ROMANS 12:2

SHOWING UNUSUAL KINDNESS

Heading into the 2014 season, Cincinnati Bengals defensive tackle Devon Still received bad news—he hadn't made the team. But head coach Marvin Lewis wanted Still to know that if he cleared waivers, the team would re-sign him to the practice squad. That meant Still would continue to receive a paycheck and health insurance.

Those details were of utmost importance to Still, given that his four-year-old daughter, Leah, had been diagnosed with stage 4 neuroblastoma, a rare form of cancer, the previous June. The team had already shown understanding, allowing Still to leave training camp to spend time with her. But signing Still to the practice squad so he could keep his insurance coverage went above and beyond the normal dog-eat-dog, results-oriented business of football.

"I'm not going to lie," Still told an Associated Press reporter. "I thought just like everybody else: This is a business. For them to be behind me this much is amazing to me and it's definitely changed my perspective on the world of sports."

Wouldn't it be nice if more people showed unusual kindness? The apostle Paul and his traveling companion Luke once experienced a similar mercy from people they didn't even know. After being shipwrecked off the coast of Malta, "the islanders showed us unusual kindness," Luke wrote. "They built a fire and welcomed us all because it was raining and cold" (Acts 28:2).

The kindness of the Maltese people allowed Paul and Luke to recover, and eventually to minister another day. And the Cincinnati Bengals' kindness gave Devon Still another chance. He remained on the practice squad for a couple of weeks until the Bengals promoted him to the active roster. Leah underwent surgery in September 2014 and finished her last cancer treatment in early 2016, with a cancer-free prognosis.

Dear friend, you are faithful in what you are doing for the brothers and sisters, even though they are strangers to you.
3 John 1:5

JOY IN TRIALS

There's no way to sugarcoat it: The 1940 NFL championship game between the Chicago Bears and the Washington Redskins was a good, old-fashioned beat-down.

On December 8, 1940, Hall of Fame coach George Halas brought his Bears to the nation's capital for the NFL's eighth annual championship. The game, a rematch of a 7–3 Redskins win three weeks earlier, was greatly anticipated. More than thirty-six thousand fans poured into Griffith Stadium to watch. And it was the first NFL championship ever broadcast nationally on radio.

No one expected the outcome.

The underdog Bears romped to a 28–0 halftime lead, intercepted eight passes (returning three for touchdowns) and won 73–0. . .the largest margin of victory in NFL history. By the fourth quarter, the Bears had kicked all the game balls into the stands on point-after attempts, forcing officials to finish the game with practice balls.

For Washington, it was a miserable end to an otherwise fantastic season. Asked if a dropped touchdown pass early in the first quarter would have changed the game, Redskins quarterback "Slingin' Sammy" Baugh answered, "Yeah, it would have made it 73–7."

The game was certainly the career nadir for many Redskins players and coaches. After all, trials aren't fun. The natural human tendency is to want difficulties to end as soon as possible.

But scripture encourages Christians not only to tolerate trials but to *rejoice* in them. Today's verse says believers are to consider life's challenges as "pure joy." And in Romans 5:3, the apostle Paul says followers of Jesus are to "glory in our sufferings." Why? Because trials help us develop faith, hope, perseverance, and other godly qualities.

You don't have to throw a party when trials come. But the proper perspective on life's hardships can help you to endure and grow spiritually.

Consider it pure joy, my brothers and sisters,
whenever you face trials of many kinds.
JAMES 1:2

"WHAT DID YOU DO THAT FOR?"

In late 2013, when college bowl game pairings were announced, many fans and sportswriters took special note of the Orange Bowl match-up between Clemson and Ohio State. The January 3, 2014, game would be only the second gridiron battle between the schools, the first in the thirty-five years since Buckeye coach Woody Hayes punched Tiger nose guard Charlie Bauman.

The shocking event occurred late in the 1978 Gator Bowl. Seventh-ranked Clemson led No. 20 Ohio State 17–15 with two minutes to play. The Buckeyes, behind freshman quarterback Art Schlichter, had driven to the Tiger 24, within range of a game-winning field goal. But on third and five, Schlichter was pressured into a bad pass that Bauman intercepted. Schlichter ultimately tackled Bauman near the Ohio State coach, who grabbed his Clemson opponent's jersey and swung at his throat. Bauman was heard saying to Hayes, "What did you do that for?"

Within a day, Hayes was fired. Twenty-eight years as the Buckeye head coach, a 205–61–10 record, thirteen Big Ten championships, and five national championships (1954, '57, '61, '68, and '70) were cast aside by a single angry outburst.

Uncontrolled anger is on a long list of "acts of the flesh" in Galatians 5:19–21, the opposite of the "fruit of the Spirit" in verses 22–23. Off-limits for Christians are "hatred, discord, jealousy, [and] fits of rage." The apostle Paul warned readers that "those who live like this will not inherit the kingdom of God."

Though even Jesus became angry (see Matthew 21:12–13), none of us are Jesus. Better to follow the wisdom of James 1:19–20: "Everyone should be. . .slow to become angry, because human anger does not produce the righteousness that God desires."

"In your anger do not sin":
Do not let the sun go down while you are still angry.
EPHESIANS 4:26

THE SUBSTITUTION OF A LIFETIME

What a way to bring in the New Year.

On January 1, 2012, with home-field advantage already secured, the Green Bay Packers rested star quarterback Aaron Rodgers and started backup Matt Flynn against the Detroit Lions.

What transpired in the regular-season finale was one of the greatest substitute performances in NFL history.

In only the second start of his pro career, the twenty-six-year-old Flynn set franchise records by passing for 480 yards and six touchdowns in a wild 45–41 victory. Despite a wind chill factor that dipped into the teens at Lambeau Field, Flynn completed 70 percent of his attempts and hit end-zone pay dirt on completions of 4, 7, 35, 36, 58 and 80 yards.

His super-sub performance also transformed him into a hot free agent target that off-season. He eventually signed with Seattle for $26 million over three years.

As great as Flynn's efforts were that day, there is someone whose work as a substitute far exceeds anything accomplished on an NFL field. Jesus Christ is the greatest substitute in the history of the world.

When the sinless Son of God sacrificed himself on the cross, He completely fulfilled the Old Testament law (Matthew 5:17), which required the shedding of innocent blood for the forgiveness of human sins (Hebrews 9:22). He suffered greatly to free you from God's terrible wrath toward sin and purchase your salvation. The price He paid made it possible for you to enjoy all the benefits of close, personal fellowship with the God who created you in His own image—both now and forever—if you put your faith in Christ.

What a substitute! What a Savior!

God presented Christ as a sacrifice of atonement,
through the shedding of his blood—to be received by faith.
ROMANS 3:25

COREY LYNCH, SAFETY

Born May 7, 1985, in Cape Coral, Florida

Played for Appalachian State Mountaineers (2003–07)

Southern Conference Defensive Player of the Year (2007)

Sixth-round pick in NFL Draft by Cincinnati Bengals (2008)

Played for Bengals (2008), Buccaneers (2009–11), Chargers (2012), Colts and Titans (2013)

6', 210 pounds

Married to a granddaughter of Billy Graham

"It's the brevity of life, you know? The Bible says that life is but a vapor. We drive three-thousand-pound cars around every day. It kind of wakes you up and makes you think about life longer and harder. Life is but a vapor." (after pulling an injured woman from a wrecked vehicle)

KEEP DISAPPOINTMENT IN PERSPECTIVE

Forty-seven-yard field goals are hardly a given, even for an NFL kicker ranked highly for accuracy. In a seven-year career, Scott Norwood made 37 field goals of 40–49 yards. . .but he's best known for one he missed.

In 1991, with eight seconds remaining in Super Bowl XXV, Norwood's teammates held hands on the Buffalo sideline. The New York Giants led 20–19, but a Bills victory rested on Norwood's leg. He got off a strong kick but the ball drifted right—and Buffalo's dream of winning its first Super Bowl vanished. One season later, the Bills released Norwood and he retired at thirty-one.

Norwood eventually became a financial planner, then a real estate agent. And over the course of time—difficult as it was to realize that most everyone he met was thinking about his failure—a new perspective began to take shape. Rather than focusing on what he'd missed, he appreciated what he had: his new career, his wife, his three children.

"If everything always worked out for you, then you don't have that sense of appreciation," Norwood told *Sports Illustrated*. "You can always think you understand what it means to have things not work out, but until you live it, you don't really know." The *SI* writer asked, "How can you measure the health and happiness of three beautiful children against a field goal?"

Indeed.

Trouble is guaranteed in this world, and—given the world's dislike for Christians—Jesus promised we can expect even more: "In this world you will have trouble," He said. But He also offered a solution: "Take heart! I have overcome the world" (John 16:33).

Don't focus on your disappointments. Keep your eyes on Jesus.

"Take my yoke upon you and learn from me, for I am gentle and humble in heart, and you will find rest for your souls. For my yoke is easy and my burden is light."
MATTHEW 11:29–30

CONSISTENCY, IN FOOTBALL AND LIFE

Football, like life in general, requires planning, attention to detail, and consistent preparation in order to be successful. Without those things, even the most talented teams can fail to play up to their potential, resulting in disappointment among the players, coaches, and fans.

Going into the 2013 college football season, the University of Alabama was expected to challenge for a third straight national championship. But along the way, head coach Nick Saban's Crimson Tide stumbled—twice—and failed to earn a spot in the championship game.

Coach Saban, always on the lookout for teachable moments, took the sting of the two-loss season and used it to motivate his talented team heading into the 2014 campaign.

Above every Tide player's locker in the Alabama locker room hung a poster bearing this motivational message: "If you continue to do the same thing that you have always done, you will get the same result. Guaranteed." And at the bottom of the poster was "0–2," in reference to Alabama's consecutive losses to archrival Auburn and Sugar Bowl opponent Oklahoma to end the 2013 season.

Coach Saban has been quick to point out that this guarantee cuts both ways. If his coaching staff and players consistently do what they know will bring them success, then they will enjoy the kind of success Alabama fans have come to expect. If they don't. . .well, then they can't expect to play up to their abilities and challenge for the national championship.

The Bible contains a message very much like the one the Alabama players see before and after every practice. When we daily live the life God calls us to live, when we honor Him in all we do, then we can expect a great result—guaranteed!

Therefore, my dear brothers and sisters, stand firm.
Let nothing move you. Always give yourselves fully to the work of the Lord,
because you know that your labor in the Lord is not in vain.
1 Corinthians 15:58

THE SOUND OF EMPATHY

More than 230 pounds of muscle combined with fine-tuned skill gave him access to the NFL. Being deaf made him an overcomer. For Seattle Seahawk Derrick Coleman, a handicap was just something to deal with. Excuses wouldn't do.

As the running back reached Super Bowl XLVIII, he had much to be proud of. . .and even more when the Seahawks' 43–8 steamrolling of Denver netted Coleman a highly prized ring. As exciting as the game was, however, we can look further to another experience with great impact.

Enter nine-year-old twins Riley and Erin Kovalcik. They'd been inspired by Coleman in a Duracell television commercial since they, too, were hearing impaired. The girls contacted Coleman and urged him to keep doing his best. He said he would.

But the story doesn't end there. Duracell and *Good Morning America* planned a special meeting between Coleman and the girls. The twins participated in a television interview before Coleman himself walked in and personally invited the whole Kovalcik family to be his guests at the Super Bowl.

Because he could understand what they faced and the struggle of being misunderstood, the football star offered empathy to the twins. . .like the apostle Paul urged all of us to do in Galatians 6:2: "Carry each other's burdens, and in this way you will fulfill the law of Christ."

Carrying burdens is why Jesus came. In becoming a man, He understood what it was like to be one of us. He offers something much better than Super Bowl tickets: daily encouragement and access to God's mercy and grace. Jesus' perfection allows Him to extend all the benefits of love and forgiveness for this life, along with an incredible "retirement plan" for eternity.

For we do not have a high priest who is unable to empathize with our weaknesses, but we have one who has been tempted in every way, just as we are—yet he did not sin.
Hebrews 4:15

FALLING DOWN...AND GETTING BACK UP

Roy Riegels is best known as the University of California player who ran 69 yards *the wrong way* in the first half of the 1929 Rose Bowl against Georgia Tech, leading to a two-point safety and an 8–7 loss to the Yellow Jackets.

Riegels's infamous wrong-way run took place in the second quarter. He had scooped up a fumble by Tech's Jack Thomason and somehow lost his bearings. He reversed field and raced 69 yards before his teammate Benny Lom caught up with him and tried to get him turned around. Reigels was swarmed under by Tech players, who stopped him at the California one-yard line. The Bears attempted to punt on the next play, and Yellow Jacket Vance Maree blocked Lom's punt, giving Georgia Tech a safety and a 2–0 lead.

At halftime, Riegels was so distraught that he told his coach, Nibs Price, that he didn't have it in him to go back out for the second half. "Coach, I can't do it," Riegels said. "I've ruined you, I've ruined myself, I've ruined the University of California. I couldn't face that crowd to save my life."

But Coach Price would have none of it. "Roy, get up and go back out there," he said, "The game is only half over."

With Coach Price's encouragement, Riegels not only managed to go back out for the remainder of the Rose Bowl, but also had an outstanding second half. Unfortunately, though, Cal ended up losing by a single point.

When you've gone the wrong way in life and are so distraught that you feel like giving up, remember Roy Riegels. And don't forget to pray that God will send you your own personal Nibs Price to help pick you up and get you headed in the right direction.

Therefore encourage one another and build each other up,
just as in fact you are doing.
1 THESSALONIANS 5:11

FOUR!

There are precious few ways to score exactly four points in a football game. So how many times has an NFL team done that?

According to the website Pro-Football-Reference.com, in its summary of "All Game Scores in NFL History" (covering nearly sixteen thousand match-ups through 2015), the answer is. . .*once.*

Generally, only history whizzes recognize the teams involved: the Chicago Cardinals fell 10–4 to the Racine Legion on November 25, 1923. In the NFL's second year of existence, the Cardinals—who would later migrate to St. Louis and Arizona—posted the league's first and so far only four-point finish.

Racine quarterback "Shorty" Barr scored six of his team's 10 points, as well as Chicago's total when he was caught twice in the end zone.

Four is an unusual number in football. . .and it took the biblical king Nebuchadnezzar by surprise, too. The powerful ruler had erected a giant golden statue, ordering everyone in Babylon to bow before it. When three Jewish exiles—Shadrach, Meshach, and Abednego—refused, the furious king had them thrown into a "fiery furnace," possibly a brick kiln.

The men were unfazed—and the king sensed something miraculous. "Nebuchadnezzar leaped to his feet in amazement and asked his advisers, 'Weren't there three men that we tied up and threw into the fire?' They replied, 'Certainly, Your Majesty.' He said, 'Look! I see four men walking around in the fire, unbound and unharmed, and the fourth looks like a son of the gods'" (Daniel 3:24–25). The King James Version has King Nebuchadnezzar saying, "The fourth is like the Son of God."

Whether or not Nebuchadnezzar recognized the Son of God, it's true that Jesus goes through every trial with His people. The Son of God, the Father, the Holy Spirit, and you. . .that's a "four" that just can't lose.

God has said, "Never will I leave you; never will I forsake you."
HEBREWS 13:5

THEY REALLY ARE VICTORS

The University of Michigan isn't just blowing smoke with its fight song. "The Victors" dates to 1898—and the football team has really backed it up over the years.

The Wolverines own the winningest program in college football. Entering the 2014 season they had 910 wins against 321 losses (with 36 ties) all-time. Notre Dame, at 874–305–42, is slightly ahead in winning percentage (.733 to .732), but when it comes to sheer excellence, victories by the hundreds, and titles by the dozens, no one tops Michigan.

Since their first intercollegiate game in 1879, the Wolverines have won or shared forty-two conference championships and earned eleven national titles. They have finished in the Top 10 thirty-seven times. Maybe that's why Michigan fans love to sing, "Hail! to the victors valiant / Hail! to the conquering heroes / Hail! Hail! to Michigan the leaders and best."

In the Bible, you'll find a doctrine of victory. It revolves around Jesus Christ and the believer's relationship with Him. Here is its central truth: "Everyone born of God overcomes the world. This is the victory that has overcome the world, even our faith" (1 John 5:4).

There is a conquering character about Christ. The world, the flesh, and the devil are all subject to Him. We prevail through Him, as Revelation 12:11 indicates: "They triumphed over [Satan] by the blood of the Lamb and by the word of their testimony."

Overcoming is in Jesus' nature. He stands in ultimate victory. He has swallowed up death and removed its sting. He is coming back again and He will *not* come in a spirit of defeat.

And those of us who follow Jesus get to enjoy the benefits of His leadership. We really are victors!

But thanks be to God!
He gives us the victory through our Lord Jesus Christ.
1 Corinthians 15:57

MR. IRRELEVANT?

If you're enough of a football freak to remain tuned in to the annual NFL Draft through the very last pick, then you're probably familiar with "Mr. Irrelevant." He's the very last pick of the draft, and he's called Mr. Irrelevant because his chances of making the team are statistically very slim.

The online *Merriam-Webster Dictionary* defines the word *irrelevant* as "not important or relating to what is being discussed right now." In the context of the NFL Draft, you could say this means that the final pick in the draft isn't considered important, simply because he'll likely never play in the league.

However, there are a few instances in the history of the NFL Draft when Mr. Irrelevant made himself relevant. Here are some of the recent highlights:

- In 1994, the New England Patriots took University of Kentucky linebacker Marty Moore, and he played 112 games in eight NFL seasons.
- In 1999, the Chicago Bears drafted University of Pennsylvania fullback Jim Finn with the very last pick, and he played 106 games in seven seasons.
- In 2000, the Bears took defensive back Michael Green with the final pick in the draft, and he played 104 games in eight seasons—six with the Bears, two with the Seattle Seahawks, and one with the Washington Redskins.

These players—and a few others throughout NFL history—may have been tagged as "irrelevant," but they were given the one thing every draft pick, from the first-rounders on down, was given: an opportunity.

When God gives us an opportunity to accomplish something—even if it seems humanly unlikely we'll really make it happen—then it's on us to take advantage and then do everything we can to succeed, including relying on Him to give us the strength and wisdom to do it.

Make the most of every opportunity in these evil days.
Don't act thoughtlessly, but understand what the Lord wants you to do.
EPHESIANS 5:16–17 NLT

WORK IN PROGRESS

If ever there was an example of a successful work in progress in the NFL, it was the 2011 New York Giants.

The Giants entered the season with high expectations but floundered to a 7–7 record after a Week 15 loss to NFC East rival Washington. Even though they won their last two games to qualify for the playoffs, the Giants entered the postseason as the least impressive division winner, having scored fewer points (394) than they had allowed (400).

But then the Giants caught fire, rattling off impressive playoff wins over Atlanta (10–6), Green Bay (15–1), and San Francisco (13–3) to reach Super Bowl XLVI, where they stunned heavily favored New England, 21–17.

The Giants ended the 2011 season as a completely different team than when the season began. Christians go through a similar experience of maturation called sanctification. It's the process where we, from the moment we are saved until death, grow to become more and more like Jesus.

In Philippians 3:13, the apostle Paul describes sanctification as "forgetting what is behind and straining toward what is ahead." As we study God's Word, apply it to our lives, and grow in our love for the Savior, we desire sin less and godliness more.

Ultimately, sanctification is a work of Jesus, the "perfecter of faith" (Hebrews 12:2), and the Holy Spirit (see 2 Thessalonians 2:13). But our efforts here matter, too. Hebrews 12:14 exhorts us to "make every effort. . .to be holy," while 1 Peter 2:11 instructs us to "abstain from sinful desires."

Here's the best part: While the 2011 Giants weren't assured a Super Bowl victory, the Bible guarantees sanctification for all believers. As Philippians 1:6 says, "He who began a good work in you will carry it on to completion until the day of Christ Jesus."

Sanctification is a guaranteed win!

And we all, who with unveiled faces contemplate the Lord's glory,
are being transformed into his image with ever-increasing glory,
which comes from the Lord, who is the Spirit.
2 CORINTHIANS 3:18

NOTRE DAME GOLD

In 2011 Notre Dame unveiled a new football helmet, one that came closer to matching the appearance of the Golden Dome landmark on campus. The color of the helmet with 23.9-karat gold flake was said to be more like that of the Golden Dome, which sits majestically atop the Main Building after a 2005 re-gilding, when it was covered by a fistful of gold leaf.

God likes gold. It reminds us of His glory and beauty. When Solomon built a temple on earth, it was a symbol of God's heavenly temple. And it featured a lot of gold. The inside of the temple, the inner sanctuary and the chains that stretched in front of it, and the altar all were overlaid with gold (see 1 Kings 6:20–22).

Gold is known as a noble element. That means it stands apart, barely reacting with the other elements. In this, it ought to remind us of how God the Father stands apart from us in such a way that we ought to revere Him.

Of course, the Bible teaches us that its words are better than gold (see Psalm 119:72). This ought to be our primary consideration as we approach our daily decisions and, particularly, the long-range choices we make for our lives.

But gold is still significant. It exists to remind us that we have a big God. He is so big that He created the players who wear the golden helmets, the athletes in other sports, and the galaxies. God created so many plant and animal species, and put them in so many lands and oceans, that they by their very existence might glorify His name. A big God put the sun precisely where it is so that we would neither melt nor freeze. A big God did all this.

A big God who likes gold.

The great street of the city was of gold, as pure as transparent glass.
Revelation 21:21

A PATH SELDOM TRAVELED

Most visitors to the Pro Football Hall of Fame in Canton, Ohio, don't give it a lot of thought, but currently ten players are enshrined there who carry an unusual distinction, namely that they were not selected in the National Football League Draft.

Perhaps the best known of those players is quarterback Warren Moon, who played three seasons of college ball at the University of Washington, where he closed out his career earning the Most Valuable Player award after leading the Huskies to the Rose Bowl championship in 1978.

But come Draft Day in 1978, Moon's name wasn't called. Moon, though, had an alternate plan—an alternate *path*. He moved north and spent six seasons playing—spectacularly—for the Canadian Football League's Edmonton Eskimos, leading them to five straight Grey Cup championships (1978 to 1982).

Though Moon enjoyed six great seasons in Canada, he never gave up on his dream of playing in the NFL. His success with the Eskimos caught the attention of NFL executives, and several teams lined up to bid for his services. He signed with the Houston Oilers in 1984. He played ten seasons in Houston, three with the Minnesota Vikings, two with the Seattle Seahawks, and two with the Kansas City Chiefs.

In his seventeen NFL seasons, Moon passed for an impressive 49,325 yards and 291 touchdowns. He played in the Pro Bowl nine times, was chosen All-Pro three times, and was enshrined in the Hall of Fame in 2006.

God may have revealed what He wants you to do, where He wants you to go, and how He wants to bless you. But if He hasn't yet revealed the path He's mapped out for you to get there, just take heart, keep trusting and working, and know that He has every step planned out for you.

In their hearts humans plan their course,
but the Lord establishes their steps.
PROVERBS 16:9

IT'S UP AND IT'S...

When the Denver Broncos' Matt Prater booted a 64-yard field goal against Tennessee on December 8, 2013, he broke a distance record that had stood for forty-three years.

Though the previous mark of 63 yards had been matched three times—by Denver's Jason Elam in 1998, Oakland's Sebastian Janikowski in 2011, and San Francisco's David Akers in 2012—it was New Orleans kicker Tom Dempsey who had set the standard on November 8, 1970. The Saints rode Dempsey's foot to a last-second, 19–17 victory over the Detroit Lions.

The record-setter obliterated the previous mark of 56 yards, set by the Baltimore Colts' Bert Rechichar in 1953, and was all the more remarkable for Dempsey's physical disability. Called "Stump" or "Stumpy" by coaches and fans, Dempsey had been born without fingers on his right hand—or toes on his right, kicking, foot. He wore a specially made, flat-faced shoe, using a straight-on, rather than soccer style, approach.

Tom Dempsey's physical imperfection didn't stop him from trying—or succeeding in—professional football. Nor should our own imperfections keep us from serving God.

After the apostle Paul enjoyed an amazing vision of heaven, the Lord allowed a "thorn in [Paul's] flesh" (2 Corinthians 12:7) to keep him humble. After Paul pleaded for its removal, God told him, "My grace is sufficient for you, for my power is made perfect in weakness" (2 Corinthians 12:9).

So, Paul concluded, "I will boast all the more gladly about my weaknesses, so that Christ's power may rest on me. . . . When I am weak, then I am strong" (2 Corinthians 12:9–10).

> *As a father has compassion on his children, so the LORD*
> *has compassion on those who fear him; for he knows how*
> *we are formed, he remembers that we are dust.*
> PSALM 103:13–14

STAND TALL

How a football team handles defeat is one of the more thought-provoking themes in the 2014 movie *When the Game Stands Tall*.

De La Salle High School in Concord, California, won 151 consecutive games before losing. It stands as the longest winning streak in high school football, and it could have been presented as the movie's main theme—win after win, season after season, climbing to the top and staying there. . .that sort of thing.

Instead the movie portrays the exact opposite. In a shocking chronology of humility, it manages to portray De La Salle as underdogs fighting for scraps of respect. The loss that ended the streak is deeply felt, and events that define the team's post-streak character are vividly set against the frailty of human striving. De La Salle is shown for what it is—a team short on depth, confidence, and maybe even talent at certain positions. The focus then becomes, "How does De La Salle fight?" Very well, thank you.

Making history with a long winning streak is not easy. Time after time, De La Salle did not falter when faced with trouble. Winning requires strength, and confidence gives birth to more confidence. But then comes the day when it all falls to pieces. What then? On the road to winning again, the De La Salle players learned just how much strength they really had.

Perfect effort is the goal. A by-product of that can be winning.

De La Salle coach Bob Ladouceur becomes known through the movie as the preacher of perfect effort "from snap to whistle." Control your perfect effort. Give it!

Above all else, we learn that De La Salle football is a brotherhood. Christians who discover perfect love have an opportunity to learn what that means (see 1 John 4:18).

If you falter in a time of trouble, how small is your strength!
Proverbs 24:10

LEADERS WHO SERVE

Since 1969, the Pittsburgh Steelers have had just three head coaches—Chuck Noll (1969–91), Bill Cowher (1992–2006), and Mike Tomlin (2007–present). Since 1969, they have gone to the playoffs twenty-eight times and won six Super Bowls.

To put that into perspective, the Steelers (who date to 1933, when they were known as the Pirates) had never won a postseason game before these coaches were at the helm. All three men have left a mark on the city of Pittsburgh and the lives of hundreds of players.

Noll took a perennial loser and used the draft to build a powerhouse, in blue-collar fashion. He didn't write books or endorse products. He was simply a quiet, solid fixture who knew how to lead. Tony Dungy, who coached under Noll, describes Noll as one of the greatest leaders he's ever been around.

Cowher, a passionate coach who loved his players, picked up where Noll left off. The 1992 AP NFL Coach of the Year held players to a high standard and today, as a broadcaster, continues to do so. He says players are role models. In one recent interview, he said playing in the NFL is a privilege and that players need to treat it as such.

Tomlin kept many of Cowher's assistant coaches in place when he took over, and he quickly became a part of the Pittsburgh community. In 2013, the Chuck Cooper Foundation recognized him and his wife, Kiya, with the Career Achievement in Leadership Diversity and Community Service Award.

The Steelers have chosen leaders who serve, just as Luke 22:26 suggests: "The greatest among you should be like the youngest, and the one who rules like the one who serves."

Where can you show leadership—by serving—today?

"I know your deeds, your love and faith, your service and perseverance, and that you are now doing more than you did at first."
REVELATION 2:19

FILLING A NEED

If you've seen the outstanding movie *The Blind Side*, then you are familiar with the story of Michael Oher (or at least the Hollywood version of it). Oher is now an offensive lineman in the National Football League.

Growing up, Michael received more than his share of hard knocks. He was one of twelve children born to an alcoholic, drug-addicted mother, and his father was in and out of prison. Michael spent time living in several foster homes—or was homeless altogether. He attended eleven different schools through his freshman year in high school and performed poorly at each one.

Enter Leigh Anne and Sean Tuohy, a well-to-do couple living in Memphis, Tennessee—Michael's hometown. Through a series of events, many of them orchestrated by Leigh Anne herself, Michel wound up not just living with the Tuohy family but actually becoming a part of the family through legal adoption.

That was a huge commitment in that the Tuohys gave not only of their ample financial resources, but of themselves. To this day, they will tell you that they love Michael just as much as they love their own biological children.

In an interview on ABC's *20/20*, Leigh Anne talked about her family's reason for bringing Michael into their family: "It had nothing to do with what color Michael was or how big he was. He was a child that had a need, and it needed to be filled."

Sometimes it's just that simple, isn't it? We see a need (or maybe even ask God to reveal one to us) and, acting out of God's love for others, extend ourselves—our efforts, our money, our own hearts—to another.

"I was hungry and you gave me something to eat, I was thirsty and you gave me something to drink, I was a stranger and you invited me in, I needed clothes and you clothed me, I was sick and you looked after me, I was in prison and you came to visit me."
MATTHEW 25:35–36

INTEGRITY IN A STRIPED UNIFORM

Most football fans aren't prone to thinking of the officials who work their favorite teams' games as men of integrity. But both the NCAA and NFL go to incredible lengths to ensure that the men who wear the stripes are people of high character and professionalism.

Football officials who work at the major college or professional levels undergo extensive background checks (even established NFL officials regularly go through FBI background checks) and must adhere to strict codes of conduct. Not only that, all officials at that level are required to know the rules and penalties for breaking those rules so well that they become second nature.

So if the NCAA and NFL put their game officials under so much scrutiny and through so much training, why do they still blow calls—and sometimes at key points in games? The answer is simply this: though they're the best at what they do, they're still human.

Jerry Markbreit, who officiated in the NFL for thirty-three seasons and who worked as the referee (the lead official) in four Super Bowls, once said, "There's no such thing as perfection. Mistakes happen. Officials are so hard on themselves. When they make a mistake, nobody feels worse than they do."

A life of integrity isn't necessarily a life free of mistakes, bad decisions, or sinful actions or thoughts. Just as football officials blow it from time to time, we're going to fail occasionally to live up to the standards God has set for us.

A life of integrity simply means that we know what God expects of us and that we make living a godly life our top priority. But when we blow it—and we all do—our God is much more willing to forgive than any slighted football fan!

Whoever walks in integrity walks securely,
but whoever takes crooked paths will be found out.
PROVERBS 10:9

JOHNATHAN FRANKLIN, RUNNING BACK

Born October 23, 1989, in Los Angeles, California

Played for UCLA Bruins (2009–12)

First-team All-American (2012)

Fourth-round pick in NFL Draft by Green Bay Packers (2013)

Played for Packers (2013)

5'10", 205 pounds

Suffered career-ending injury in first NFL season

"Our God has a purpose, and paths set for all of us. . . . I understand God knows what he is doing and for now he has another platform for me to step upon. I ask that you all pray for me during this transition, I will stay strong and keep my peace through Christ because he is my guider." (Tweet after announcing his departure from the NFL)

THE RIGHT CALL

With tears streaming down his cheeks, the six-foot-six-inch, 266-pound defensive monster from South Carolina hugged family members, took a deep breath, and made his way from the backstage area to the center-stage podium.

Moments earlier, NFL commissioner Roger Goodell had announced Jadeveon Clowney as the first overall pick of the 2014 NFL Draft in New York City. And the big guy wept like a baby.

The calling of players in one of America's most hyped sporting events has produced some memorable moments over the years. Remember when quarterback Robert Griffin III, the Washington Redskins' second overall selection in 2012, pulled up his left pant leg to reveal burgundy and gold socks? And who can forget quarterback Johnny Manziel's trademark "show me the money" finger-rub after the Cleveland Browns took him with their first-round pick in 2014?

Christians have been called, too. . .but this calling is far greater. While many NFL teams wait until the last minute on draft night to make their selections, the Bible says God planned each believer's spiritual calling before time began.

The New Testament is filled with references to God's election—or "predestination"—and calling of believers. (See Romans 8:28; 1 Corinthians 1:9; Ephesians 1:4; 1 Thessalonians 1:4; 2 Thessalonians 2:13; 2 Timothy 1:9; 1 Peter 2:9; and 2 Peter 1:3.)

But perhaps no passage summarizes the Christian's calling and God-directed salvation process better than Romans 8:30, shown below. When God calls those He has already predestined, He changes their sinful hearts to receive the Gospel. This calling never fails—it always results in justification (being made right with God through saving faith in Jesus) and glorification (eternal life in heaven).

God's calling is a wonderful, mysterious act of His amazing grace.

And those he predestined, he also called; those he called,
he also justified; those he justified, he also glorified.
ROMANS 8:30

HALLS OF FAME

If you travel Interstate 77 through Canton, Ohio, you'll probably notice the Pro Football Hall of Fame on the west side of the highway. It's hard to miss—the original building, now the main entrance to a complex of structures, looks like an orange juicer with its football-shaped dome.

In 1959, Canton's newspaper, the *Repository*, kicked off a campaign for the hall with an editorial entitled PRO FOOTBALL NEEDS A HALL OF FAME AND LOGICAL SITE IS HERE. The logic included the fact that the American Professional Football Association, later renamed the National Football League, was organized in Canton in 1920. And the first two-time NFL champion—in 1922 and 1923—was the Canton Bulldogs, a team that once featured football legend Jim Thorpe.

Canton's bid was successful, and the facility opened September 7, 1963, with a class of seventeen inductees. Besides Thorpe, they included quarterback Sammy Baugh, halfback Red Grange (the "Galloping Ghost"), fullback Bronko Nagurski, tackle Cal Hubbard, and team founders and coaches George Halas and Curly Lambeau.

The Bible contains a "Faith Hall of Fame" in Hebrews 11, highlighting characters such as Noah, Abraham, Moses, and Joshua. The familiar chapter provides powerful examples for us to emulate—though the fact is that the great majority of us will never rise to their level. Whether in the NFL or the Bible, halls of fame are exclusive places reserved for people of great visibility.

But always remember that whatever good you do is visible to the most important Audience of all: God Himself. In the parable of the talents (or "bags of gold," in the updated New International Version), basic obedience results in the Lord's blessing: "Well done, good and faithful servant! You have been faithful with a few things; I will put you in charge of many things. Come and share your master's happiness!" (Matthew 25:21).

That's better than any human fame.

"Those who honor me I will honor."
1 SAMUEL 2:30

CHEST UP, EYES UP, PRAYED UP

If you had a chance to meet Pittsburgh Steelers wide receiver Antonio Brown in person, one of the first things you might notice about him is that he has a gift for encouraging others—a gift he even turns on himself, using his personal slogan: "Chest Up. Eyes Up. Prayed Up"—CUEUPU for short.

Brown says he coined his own personal mantra as a way to inspire himself—as a football player, as a father, and as a man who spends much of his free time working with charities in the Pittsburgh area, including Big Brothers Big Sisters of Greater Pittsburgh. "It's a constant reminder that if I live with my chest up and my eyes up, and I'm prayed up, I can handle anything life throws at me," he said.

And life has thrown plenty at Antonio Brown. He grew up in the Liberty City area of northwest Miami, Florida, an area notorious for crime, violence, drugs, and poverty. Growing up, Brown had little to call his own, including a home for a time.

But don't ask him to complain or lament his background. Instead, he prefers to take encouragement and motivation not just from his own personal slogan, but also from the encouraging, strengthening words of the Bible. That's what keeps him going—and what allows him to serve as an encouragement for so many in the Pittsburgh area.

Most of us didn't have it as rough as Antonio Brown as we were growing up. But that doesn't mean that life won't throw us our share of difficulties. But when it does, we can take heart from Antonio's example, the encouragement of others, and the many uplifting, encouraging messages found in the pages of scripture.

The Lord is my light and my salvation—whom shall I fear?
The Lord is the stronghold of my life—of whom shall I be afraid?
Psalm 27:1

THE BUILDUP

Two weeks is a long time to wait.

From the moment the AFC and NFC championship games end in late January, the countdown begins for the biggest sporting event in America: the Super Bowl.

The buildup to the Big Game, which was first played in January 1967, when Vince Lombardi's Green Bay Packers beat Kansas City, 35–10, has become a cultural phenomenon. Each year, the national sports media provide exhaustive coverage of every last detail of the players and teams involved. Super Bowl Media Day, the Tuesday prior to the game, is a circus unto itself.

Companies pony up millions of dollars for 30-second commercial spots during the game. Snack food sales spike nationwide as fans load up on soda, beer, chips, pretzels, ice cream, and more. And the gambling industry kicks into high gear, reaping untold millions of dollars in profits from the game.

Oftentimes, though, the pregame hype exceeds the actual contest. Take Super Bowl XLVIII, after the 2013 season, for instance. The 111.5 million TV viewers who tuned in to watch Denver vs. Seattle saw a dud of a game. The Seahawks led 22–0 by halftime and eventually won a 43–8 laugher.

As Christians, we anticipate something infinitely greater than the Super Bowl. We are awaiting the return of the Lord Jesus Christ.

When Jesus returns, He will come as a conquering warrior who will destroy evil (Revelation 19:11–21) and inaugurate "a new heaven and a new earth" (Revelation 21:1). This eternal heavenly kingdom will be free of all sadness, pain, and death (Revelation 21:4). Best of all, we will live in the glorious presence of God the Father and His Son forever (Revelation 21:3).

No one knows when Jesus will return (Matthew 24:36), but when He does, we'll be welcomed into a heaven greater than anything we can imagine. As today's verse says, come, Lord Jesus!

He who testifies to these things says,
"Yes, I am coming soon." Amen. Come, Lord Jesus.
REVELATION 22:20

RECORDS LIKE ANDERSEN'S REQUIRE STRENGTH

Welcome to NFL Earth, where records stand like mountains.

Jerry Rice (receiving yards and touchdowns) and Emmitt Smith (rushing yards and touchdowns) are two of the higher peaks. Quarterbacks like Brett Favre and Peyton Manning are also visible on the highest range. Yards gained and thrown for tend to be majestic numbers and are duly noted.

But the bottom line in the NFL is to score more points than the opposing team. For an individual to help in that process for years on end is remarkable. It is like the creation of a Mount Everest—the highest point of elevation. This is the career record for points scored, and it belongs to a kicker, Morten Andersen, and it stands at 2,544.

Andersen is a man of humble beginnings. He was a foreign exchange student from Denmark who came to the United States and discovered the art of kicking a football. A pro from 1982 through 2007, he is the only player to hold franchise scoring records for two teams (the New Orleans Saints and the Atlanta Falcons). He also holds the mark for most consecutive games scoring a point (360).

Mountains are impressive, but there are limits when men create records that stand like mountains. Typically, an NFL record holder will not take total credit for what he has accomplished. He often will attest that his talent comes from God. Said another way, he knows that he was not the One who put the mountain in place. He certainly needed help, and that was provided by the Lord.

The Lord is the strength of every life, and it is good for men to acknowledge it (see Psalm 27:1). Like blocking in football, which is not found in the record books, strength is always there. Think about how it works.

I lift up my eyes to the mountains—where does my help come from?
My help comes from the LORD, the Maker of heaven and earth.
PSALM 121:1–2

FALLING SHORT OF PERFECTION

In the days leading up to the Super Bowl XLII matchup between the New York Giants and the undefeated New England Patriots, it seemed that nearly every prognosticator had the Patriots not just winning, but winning in a rout.

A few other NFL teams had finished their seasons unbeaten, but the 2007 Patriots accomplished what no other team in NFL history had ever done, winning sixteen regular-season games to finish with a perfect record. The Pats tore through the regular season, rarely winning by less than double figures, and then followed that up with two wins in the playoffs to take their spot in the Super Bowl.

But something unexpected occurred on the way to the Pats blowing out the Giants on February 8, 2008, in Glendale, Arizona.

It didn't happen.

The Giants defense harassed record-setting Patriots quarterback Tom Brady all day long, sacking him five times, and shut down New England's running game on the way to a stunning 17–14 win that is considered one of the biggest upsets in Super Bowl history.

The Bible contains many examples of people who started out strong serving God and continuing to serve Him faithfully through most of their lives, only to fail in the end. Look up the following monarchs of Israel and Judah, just for a few examples: Solomon, Asa, Josiah, and Uzziah. All of these men served God faithfully for most of their lives, only to falter at the end.

Starting out strong is always a good thing, and continuing on that way during the middle parts of what God has called you to do and be is even better. But to get the prize God has promised, He calls us to continue on until we finish what He has called us to do.

Do you not know that in a race all the runners run,
but only one gets the prize? Run in such a way as to get the prize.
1 CORINTHIANS 9:24

FAN THE FLAMES OF FAITHFULNESS

No one is perfect, but some NFL players are faithful to do just about everything right.

In 1972, center Jim Langer of the Miami Dolphins executed 497 of his 500 blocking assignments without any help. His team is famous for recording the last perfect season in NFL history.

Langer's story is tied to his being faithful in smaller places long before he snapped his first football in the big city. He grew up in Royalton, Minnesota, and played college football in Brookings, South Dakota, for South Dakota State University.

He was not drafted following his senior season, and the Cleveland Browns waived him before he signed with the Dolphins as a free agent. Despite his humble professional beginnings, he enjoyed a Hall of Fame career, which ended with his final two seasons as a member of the Minnesota Vikings. After Langer retired, he and his wife, Linda, were faithful to guide their four children through South Dakota State and maintain close ties with the campus they love.

Langer's ability to be faithful in virtually every task he was called on to complete helped make Miami a championship team. Through it all, he remained a champion to the home folks, too. In 2001, Royalton named its football field for him.

God promises that His eyes will be on you if you are faithful (see Psalm 101:6) and that He will preserve the faithful (see Psalm 31:23). God is faithful in every way (see Deuteronomy 7:9), so He is always on the lookout for those who follow in His footsteps.

Langer's faithfulness was evident in his excellent blocking. How are you handling the tasks set before you? Can it be said of you that you are being faithful with those responsibilities?

Many claim to have unfailing love, but a faithful person who can find?
PROVERBS 20:6

PROGRESS IN SMALL DOSES

On October 19, 1985, the seventh-ranked Nebraska Cornhuskers probably expected to visit Missouri's end zone early and often in Columbia. The Tigers were winless on the season, and one Nebraska newspaper described their defense as "porous."

But the Huskers were unable to find the end zone for the first three quarters. Instead, they relied on a junior walk-on kicker, Dale Klein, who attempted and made *seven* field goals—from 32, 22, 43, 44, 29, 43, and 43 yards—helping the Huskers sneak away with a 28–20 victory. Klein tied an NCAA record set the year prior by Western Michigan's Mike Prindle, who made seven field goals while missing two in a single game. Klein is still the only kicker in history to make as many as seven field goals in one game without a miss.

The Cornhuskers undoubtedly wanted more offensive success that day, but they took field goals whenever possible—knowing that a few points are better than none. Sometimes our spiritual progress works like that. Small gains are better than no gains. Though we'd like to be perfect, we strive for progress in whatever size or shape it comes.

In Paul's first letter to Timothy, the great apostle encouraged his young charge to be an example for believers in speech, conduct, love, faith, and purity. Paul told Timothy to devote himself to the public reading of scripture, to preaching, and to teaching. "Be diligent in these matters," Paul wrote. "Give yourself wholly to them, so that everyone may see your progress" (1 Timothy 4:15).

If we're making progress, we're heading toward victory.

We continually ask God to fill you with the knowledge of his will through
all the wisdom and understanding that the Spirit gives, so that you
may live a life worthy of the Lord and please him in every way:
bearing fruit in every good work, growing in the knowledge of God.
COLOSSIANS 1:9–10

"TEAM JACK"

If the video of a seven-year-old brain cancer patient scoring a touchdown in a Nebraska spring training game doesn't bring a tear to your eye, you're way too tough.

Google it if you need to: On Saturday, April 6, 2013, young Jack Hoffman takes a fourth-and-one handoff from Huskers quarterback Taylor Martinez and races to the end zone for a touchdown. Wearing the red number 22 jersey of running back Rex Burkhead, his friend and leader of the support group "Team Jack," the boy follows his blockers 69 yards for the score. More than sixty thousand fans in Lincoln cheer wildly, and Jack is mobbed by both teams in the end zone.

The once-in-a-lifetime experience was conceived by Sooners fullback C. J. Zimmerer and director of football operations Jeff Jamrog, and left Jack's father fighting back emotion on the sidelines. "Husker fans have been so incredible to Jack and our family," Andy Hoffman said. According to the seven-year-old, "It felt awesome."

You have to believe that Jesus, who welcomed children to His side, would approve. Jack's experience brings to mind Jesus' parable in which the Lord judges the nations by separating "the sheep from the goats" (Matthew 25:32). The sheep, who are blessed by the Father and take their inheritance in the kingdom, are commended for feeding the Lord, giving Him drink, providing Him clothes and lodging, and visiting Him while sick or in prison. The righteous people don't remember ever doing such things for Jesus—but He answers, "Truly I tell you, whatever you did for one of the least of these brothers and sisters of mine, you did for me" (Matthew 25:40).

Find someone in need to serve today. You'll be serving Jesus Himself— and gain a huge blessing in return.

"If anyone gives even a cup of cold water to one of these little ones
who is my disciple, truly I tell you, that person will
certainly not lose their reward."
MATTHEW 10:42

INTEGRITY RIDES IN ON A PUNT

The word *integrity* means wholeness—not perfection but fullness, as when all the pieces fit.

Before 2014, twenty-three of twenty-four positions were represented in the NFL Hall of Fame. All eleven spots on offense and defense were there. A kicker had been voted in, too, but not a punter. Which is why the induction of former Oakland Raiders punter Ray Guy mattered.

"It's been long, long overdue, but now the Hall of Fame has a complete team," Guy said.

Integrity means handling all of the details so a presentation or a person can hold together. David knew that (see Psalm 26:1). For the punting position, which is a lowly football job, closing the chain's last link was huge. About twenty former punters came to the ceremony to witness it.

"A God-given talent is one of the greatest gifts an individual can be blessed with," Guy said. "But to use a God-given gift for just one's self is not the answer. The true benefit of a gift is to share with others. Even though I had a special talent, I was taught to keep my ego in its place. I've always been a humble person. I've never felt comfortable with attention that football brought. I'd rather be in the background, just one of the people."

A man with integrity projects confidence. David had it and Israel prospered.

The symbolism of the NFL achieving even a small measure of this through its selection of Guy was not lost on the greater punting fraternity.

"This is a rite of passage," said Jeff Feagles, who punted professionally for twenty-two years. "The position needs to be represented. Guy's induction will open a lot of eyes."

Do what you say and do hold together? Are you neglecting something obscure like punting? It's never too late to pursue integrity.

Because of my integrity you uphold me
and set me in your presence forever.
PSALM 41:12

HOW TO BE A WINNER

Hall of Fame tight end and former Chicago Bears coach Mike Ditka knows a little something about winning—and losing.

Today's National Football League fans probably remember Ditka best as the coach of the 1985 Chicago Bears, who went 15–1 in the regular season before tearing through the playoffs and blowing out New England 46–10 in Super Bowl XX.

But Ditka didn't enjoy instant success as the Bears head man. In fact, in his first year, the strike-shortened 1982 season, the Bears finished 3–6 before going 8–8 in 1983 and 10–6 in 1984. But "Iron" Mike and his Bears also went through some difficult seasons after Super Bowl XX, including a 6–10 record in 1989 and a 5–11 finish in 1992.

Ditka once gave voice to his thoughts about winning and losing when he said, "You are never a loser until you quit trying."

Wise words, indeed, words that have application in the spiritual life of one who follows Jesus Christ. You see, this world, as well as the devil himself, will put up roadblocks and discouragements as we do all we can to live the life God calls us to live. To put it in football terms, the world and our spiritual enemy do all they can to make us "losers."

The Bible teaches us that while we are to depend on God to empower us to do what He calls us to do (see Philippians 4:13), we also play our part by doing the simple things it takes to access His strength—things such as endeavoring to more fully depend on God and staying close to Him through prayer and Bible reading.

God has promised us that when we do those things, we'll be winners in the end.

Everyone born of God overcomes the world. This is the victory that has overcome the world, even our faith. Who is it that overcomes the world? Only the one who believes that Jesus is the Son of God.
1 John 5:4–5

REALIZED POTENTIAL

Gale Sayers was the youngest player ever inducted into the Pro Football Hall of Fame. While that's an impressive achievement, it happened because he left the game sooner than anyone expected.

With the Kansas Jayhawks, Sayers set an NCAA Division I record in 1963 with a 99-yard run against Nebraska. A first-round draft pick by the Chicago Bears in 1965, Sayers exploded on the pro football scene. He rewrote the record books with his 22 touchdowns, including six in one game against San Francisco. Sayers was the unanimous choice as NFL Rookie of the Year.

More success followed. Sayers led the league in rushing his sophomore season, and picked up a Pro Bowl berth. But in his fourth season, Sayers suffered an injury to his right knee. A year later, his left knee was hurt. By 1971, Sayers reluctantly retired.

"God gave me a great gift and I had a lot of help developing for this occasion," Sayers said in his 1977 Hall of Fame induction speech. "Reaching this point, however, is not as important as striving to get here. . . . Nothing is more of a waste than unrealized potential. Sometimes failure to use one's talents to the fullest is the fault of the individual."

Sayers's comments bring to mind Jesus' parable of the talents. God wants His children to be good stewards of what He gives them. In Mathew 25, Jesus describes three servants who were asked to manage their boss's wealth. Two servants used their potential to benefit their employer. But in verse 26, the master criticized the one who didn't even try, saying, "You wicked, lazy servant!"

God gives each of us tools we can use to impact our world. What particular talents or abilities do you have? How can you use them today for God's glory?

For the Spirit God gave us does not make us timid,
but gives us power, love and self-discipline.
2 TIMOTHY 1:7

FOOTBALL, CARS, AND LOVE

For an elite-level running back, Alfred Morris sure has an ordinary ride.

In 2012, Morris took the NFL by storm as a rookie for the Washington Redskins, piling up a team-record 1,613 yards rushing (the third-highest rookie total in NFL history) and 13 touchdowns. All this despite being a sixth-round draft pick out of Florida Atlantic University. His surprising production was a major reason the Redskins won their first NFC East Division title in thirteen seasons.

Yet for all the publicity the soft-spoken Morris received during his phenomenal rookie campaign, his car received plenty, too. Local and national media couldn't get enough of "Bentley," Morris's affectionately nicknamed 1991 Mazda 626, which served as an apt metaphor for a young player who avoided the trappings of instant success. *Sports Illustrated*, *USA Today*, the *Washington Post*, Yahoo! Sports, CBSSports.com, and the Washington, DC, area's NBC TV affiliate were among the many media outlets to feature the unassuming Morris and his unimpressive set of wheels.

Despite sudden fame, Morris, who grew up in a lower-class family in Pensacola, Florida, remained content with what God had given him. He knew that the things of this world are fleeting.

This should be our mind-set, too. Nothing the world offers can satisfy us.

First Timothy 6:9 says, "Those who want to get rich fall into temptation and a trap and into many foolish and harmful desires that plunge people into ruin and destruction." And 1 John 2:17 reminds us, "The world and its desires pass away, but whoever does the will of God lives forever."

God did not create us to love worldly things. He created us to love and worship Him. Be content with what God has given you and reserve your love for Him alone, not the things of this world.

Do not love the world or anything in the world.
If anyone loves the world, love for the Father is not in them.
1 John 2:15

WINNING THE DAY

Tucked up in the northwest corner of the United States, Eugene, Oregon, has become the home of a college football program that has grown from being a nice story of overachieving most of the time—and rising up with big seasons from time to time—to being a consistent national power.

The University of Oregon Ducks (not the most imposing mascot in college football!) have established themselves as contenders for some of the top high school talent in the nation, have influenced the game with their "blur" offense, and have recently put themselves squarely in the middle of conversations about national title challengers.

Oregon had enjoyed success before the arrival of Coach Chip Kelly, but he turned up the heat on college football by instilling in his players a "win the day" attitude. The results—even after Kelly left the Ducks to coach the NFL's Philadelphia Eagles—speak for themselves. Oregon played in four straight BCS bowl games, including the National Championship games following the 2010 and 2014 regular seasons, and is consistently ranked among the best in college football.

The message behind the "win the day" mantra is simple: prepare for one opponent (the next one!) at a time and focus on doing what it takes to be successful on game day. That includes everything each player does at practice every day.

Jesus preached a message with a "win the day" theme when He said, "Do not worry about tomorrow, for tomorrow will worry about itself. Each day has enough trouble of its own" (Matthew 6:34).

Jesus never said it wasn't good to plan and prepare for the future, only that life will be better for those who focus on what He has in store for them each and every day. So by all means plan and prepare, but remember that God is in control of what comes your way in the future.

Praise be to the Lord, to God our Savior, who daily bears our burdens.
PSALM 68:19

FIRST OF THE FIRST

In recent years, the NFL Draft has become an event almost as big and exciting as many games. Fans gather around televisions or hover over their devices to see who will be the number one selection, an honor many players have carried into wildly successful careers.

Consider some of these top draft picks of the past few decades: O. J. Simpson (1969, 11 years played, first player to rush 2,000 yards in a season, Hall of Fame); Terry Bradshaw (1970, 14 years played, two Super Bowl MVPs, Hall of Fame); John Elway (1983, 16 years played, 10 Pro Bowls, NFL and Super Bowl MVP, Hall of Fame); Troy Aikman (1989, 12 years played, six Pro Bowls, winningest quarterback of the 1990s, Hall of Fame), Orlando Pace (1997, 12 years played, seven Pro Bowls); Peyton Manning (1998, 18 years played, 14 Pro Bowls).

The NFL Draft dates to 1936, when a halfback—Heisman Trophy winner Jay Berwanger of the University of Chicago—became "first of the first" as choice of the Eagles. Philadelphia offered Berwanger $125 to $150 per game, good pay during the Depression years, but he declined, saying he'd rather use his education than his football skills.

The Eagles traded their rights to the Bears, whose owner, George Halas, asked Berwanger what he would need to play. The answer was a guaranteed $25,000 for two years; Halas said he couldn't afford that, but the men parted as friends. Though Berwanger never did play professional football, he will always be honored as the first man drafted by an NFL team.

A far greater honor belongs to Jesus Christ, described by the apostle Paul as "the firstborn over all creation" (Colossians 1:15). This "first of the first" distinction doesn't describe birth order—Jesus is an eternal member of the Trinity—rather, it's a term of preeminence. Paul goes on to say, "All things have been created through him and for him" (Colossians 1:16).

Jesus is truly the most important figure of all history. . .yet He gave His life for each of us. That's really something to cheer about.

He is the head of the body, the church; he is the beginning and the firstborn from among the dead, so that in everything he might have the supremacy.
COLOSSIANS 1:18

ANDY STUDEBAKER, OUTSIDE LINEBACKER

Born September 16, 1985, in Congerville, Illinois

Played for Wheaton College Thunder (2004–08)

First-team Division III All-American (2006)

Sixth-round pick in NFL Draft by Philadelphia Eagles (2008)

Played for Chiefs (2008–12), Jaguars (2013), Colts (2013–)

6'3", 255 pounds

"We all need to know where we can find our hope, and our hope needs to be in Jesus Christ. Football can't satisfy us, the paychecks can't, the expensive cars can't, and the things we love in this world can't sustain us. Only Christ can fulfill us."

A SPECIAL UNIFORM

Until the 2014 season, only six Michigan Wolverine receivers had ever worn jersey No. 1. Five of them went on to play in the NFL.

Anthony Carter (1979–82), Greg McMurtry (1986–89), Derrick Alexander (1990–93), Tyrone Butterfield (1994–96, the only non-NFL No. 1 from Michigan), David Terrell (1998–2000), and Braylon Edwards (2003–04) had donned the hallowed jersey. Carter set the bar high, being named a consensus All-American twice (1981–82) as well as the 1982 Big Ten Player of the Year. He also finished fourth in Heisman voting in '82.

Ten years after Edwards, Devin Funchess requested a change from his No. 87 jersey to the famed No. 1, but he knew that wouldn't come easy. Funchess approached team leaders during the off-season to ask if they thought he was working hard enough to earn the number. Then–Wolverines head coach Brady Hoke gave Funchess a test, asking him to name all the players who had worn the number before.

"He started with Anthony Carter and went down the list," Hoke told an ESPN.com reporter, "and I think that he has earned it." Funchess began the 2014 season, against Appalachian State, wearing No. 1 and representing a powerful Michigan tradition.

In a similar way, we as Christians want to represent our Lord well. But we could never earn our heavenly uniform, so Jesus Christ did it for us. We will get the privilege of wearing a special outfit one day, as Revelation 7:9 describes: "After this I looked, and there before me was a great multitude that no one could count, from every nation, tribe, people and language, standing before the throne and before the Lamb. They were wearing white robes."

Though Jesus did the work, we have an obligation to respect the uniform He gives us. How are you representing it today?

"The one who is victorious will. . .be dressed in white."
Revelation 3:5

INTEGRITY AND THE PURSUIT OF CHARACTER

Selected 184th in the 1947 draft, Tom Landry had a mediocre NFL playing career. Though his stats weren't impressive during his six-year playing career with the New York Giants (and one season with the New York Yankees of the All-America Football Conference), others saw Landry's potential as a coach. By 1955 he had transitioned to a reassignment off the field.

In 1960 Landry received a call from the new team in Dallas. Offered the head coaching job with the Cowboys, he accepted—and after twenty-nine years had 270 victories, a coaching record that trails only Don Shula and George Halas.

But beyond winning games, Landry had an intense interest in developing player integrity. Landry didn't like the idea of *motivating* players; he told them simple truth (such as "A winner never stops trying,") and let it change them from the inside out.

Former Dallas receiver Drew Pearson said of Landry, "He wasn't just about building football teams. It was about building men of character. Many of the things he did were to teach us important lessons about our success in life after football."

Leadership and character building are investments in the lives of others. As the apostle Paul said to his protégé, Timothy, "The things you have heard me say in the presence of many witnesses entrust to reliable people who will also be qualified to teach others" (2 Timothy 2:2).

But developing other people is not just the job of head coaches, type-A leaders, or credentialed "experts." All of us have life experiences—informed by God's Word—that others can learn from.

Whom can you influence today?

I am not seeking my own good but the good of many, so that they may be saved. Follow my example, as I follow the example of Christ.
1 CORINTHIANS 10:31–11:1

REMEMBER THE ICE BOWL

One of the most famous games in professional football took place on the last day of 1967. The Green Bay Packers met the Dallas Cowboys in an NFL championship game that was dominated by the weather. With the temperature at –13 degrees at kickoff and the wind chill falling to –46 degrees, Lambeau Field was transformed into the "Ice Bowl."

Packers coach Vince Lombardi trusted in a system where the field could be heated by electric coils. In theory it was sound, but the Ice Bowl won out. The system failed miserably and the field was a frozen mess.

Players felt the game would be canceled and rescheduled, but the NFL determined that conditions were acceptable. This was, after all, football.

Green Bay led 14–0. The Cowboys may have been longing for home, but they fought back, stunning the Packers and taking a 17–14 lead on a trick play, a halfback option pass, in the fourth quarter.

In one of the legendary drives of pro football history, the Packers marched 68 yards to win the game 21–17. A daring quarterback plunge in the final half minute, when the Packers had no timeouts left, proved to be the difference. Lombardi later said he wanted the game to end so the fans wouldn't have to sit through an overtime.

Today, many NFL teams play in domed stadiums where conditions are always mild and calm. But for those like the Packers who still play outside, God's sovereignty over the weather remains a factor. Man can try to control it, but tundra still freezes. On any given Sunday ice can appear. Technology may help us reduce the variables in our world. . .but games like the Ice Bowl remind us that God is still the ultimate Weatherman.

"The breath of God produces ice,
and the broad waters become frozen."
Job 37:10

BE CAREFUL THAT YOU DON'T FALL

Sometimes the Super Bowl is nothing but super trouble for a player caught up in the pride that winning the game can bring.

Timmy Smith was an NFL rookie running back who had one memorable game for the Washington Redskins. In Super Bowl XXII, he rushed for 204 yards to set a record that still stood as of 2015. He also earned a Super Bowl ring as the Redskins defeated the Denver Broncos, 42–10.

But Smith's pro career after that was a bust. He was out of the league by 1990 and wound up in prison in 2006 for cocaine distribution. A court in Denver also ordered him to pay $88,000 in back child support.

"I think I got big so fast I didn't know how to respond," Smith later said.

Looking at the Timmy Smith story may be dangerous for you, if you do it with a self-righteous attitude (Ecclesiastes 7:16–18). Examining what happened to him, how he did not go on to become one of the all-time great running backs, contains peril in that you could end up believing his sins are much worse than you could ever commit. That is the pride trap you want to avoid.

Of course, wickedness is not a good option either. It is the other extreme, one you must work to avoid as well. The key to the victorious life is to fear, or revere, God. That is your means of escape.

According to news reports, Smith struggled because of his lack of discipline, partying, and hanging around with people of questionable character. You may not struggle with any of those things, but the Bible still reminds you that even if you think you are standing tall, strong, and holy, you must be careful that you don't fall (see 1 Corinthians 10:12).

It would be wrong for you to think that your sins are relatively minor compared to choices that land people in prison. All who sin need Christ (see Romans 6:23), and the Bible warns that a self-righteous man can destroy himself, too.

Pride goes before destruction, a haughty spirit before a fall.
PROVERBS 16:18

LET'S MAKE SOME NOISE!

Not every NFL battle takes place on the playing field. In 2013, a very noisy competition took place as the fans of two NFL teams battled to be listed in the *Guinness Book of World Records.*

It began in September, as the fans of the Seattle Seahawks set the world record for the loudest crowd roar. The fans at Century Link Field hit 136.6 decibels to take the record away from a Turkish soccer team. One month later, the fans of the Kansas City Chiefs bested the world record at Arrowhead Stadium. The decibel level reached 137.5 dBA.

Seahawks fans made one last attempt in December 2013. During the third quarter of Seattle's Monday Night game with the New Orleans Saints, the crowd raised its collective voice in support of its defense, and the roar reached the new record of 137.6 dBA.

According to the Guinness World Records website, the roar by the Seahawks crowd registered with the Pacific Northwest Seismic Network. The Seahawks fans—the 12th Man—had caused an earthquake!

The Holy Spirit brought the apostle John to the throne room of heaven. At the command of Christ, John recorded the scene in Revelation 4. It is a scene of complete and total worship of the One who is worthy. There is a voice like a trumpet. There are rich and vibrant colors of emerald and jasper and rubies. There are flashes of lightning and rumbles and peals of thunder. In addition, there are four magnificent creatures who never stop saying, "'Holy, holy, holy is the Lord God Almighty,' who was, and is, and is to come" (verse 8).

One day, believers will join together and praise the Lord as He sits on His throne. For now, we can join the psalmist who wrote of our obligation and opportunity while here on earth.

*Let everything that has breath praise the L*ORD.
PSALM 150:6

WISDOM FROM "THE POPE"

When a coach who has won six National Football League championships—including the first two Super Bowls—talks about what it takes to achieve success, it's probably a good idea to lend an ear.

Vince Lombardi, who coached the five-time NFL champion Green Bay Packers teams of the 1960s (and who won an NFL title as the offensive coordinator of the New York Giants), once said, "The spirit, the will to win, and the will to excel are the things that endure. These qualities are so much more important than the events that occur."

Every championship team—no matter how dominating they may appear on the field—must overcome adversity in order to win. In football, adversity comes in the form of injuries, illnesses, fatigue, days when one or more players just aren't playing their best, midseason losses, and tough calls by the men in stripes.

Mr. Lombardi—who was nicknamed "the Pope" in Green Bay—taught his teams (and anyone else who cared to listen) that champions accomplish their goals through what's in their hearts and minds, and that the will to succeed makes it possible to overcome all sorts of adversity.

It's not hard to imagine the apostle James listening to Lombardi's words from heaven and nodding in agreement. After all, he taught essentially the same thing when he wrote, "Consider it pure joy, my brothers and sisters, whenever you face trials of many kinds, because you know that the testing of your faith produces perseverance" (James 1:2–3).

God never promised believers an easy ride into heaven once they turn to Him in faith. In fact, He promised the exact opposite. The good news is that He also promised that He would be with us, working in us to make us overcomers.

"I have told you these things, so that in me you may have peace. In this world you will have trouble. But take heart! I have overcome the world."
JOHN 16:33

A GREAT NAME

He was a seventeenth-round draft pick, number 200 overall. At 6'1" and 200 pounds, he wasn't dramatically big for a quarterback. Through his first five seasons, he threw far more interceptions (40) than touchdown passes (23). His NFL future wasn't looking bright.

But Bart Starr ultimately lived up to his surname. After a college career with the Crimson Tide in his home state of Alabama, Starr was selected by Green Bay in the 1956 NFL Draft. When Vince Lombardi took over as Packers coach three years later, he helped mold Starr into one of the league's best quarterbacks—one who would lead his team to a 62–24–4 record from 1960 to '67. Behind Starr, the Packers would win six division titles, five NFL championships, and victories in Super Bowls I and II. Starr was named Most Valuable Player of each, a 35–10 win over Kansas City in 1967 and a 33–14 victory over Oakland in 1968. His record in the playoffs was a sterling 9–1.

After a sixteen-year career entirely with Green Bay, Starr earned a well-deserved spot in the Pro Football Hall of Fame. His on-field accomplishments speak for themselves—but it didn't hurt anything that Bart Starr possessed a great name, too.

An even greater name—the greatest, in fact—belongs to Jesus Christ. According to the apostle Paul, God "gave him the name that is above every name, that at the name of Jesus every knee should bow, in heaven and on earth and under the earth, and every tongue acknowledge that Jesus Christ is Lord, to the glory of God the Father" (Philippians 2:9–11).

Someday, *everyone* will agree on the greatness of Jesus' name—whether they want to or not. Why not gladly, voluntarily acknowledge Him now?

"[Mary] will give birth to a son, and you are to give him the name Jesus, because he will save his people from their sins."
MATTHEW 1:21

IT'S A MIRACLE!

Football fans know it as the "Music City Miracle."

Late in an AFC wild-card playoff game on January 8, 2000, the Buffalo Bills pulled ahead of the host Tennessee Titans, 16–15, on a 41-yard field goal. With 16 seconds remaining, the Titans' Lorenzo Neal fielded the ensuing kickoff at the 25-yard line and initiated a special teams play called "Home Run Throwback."

Neal quickly pitched the ball back to Frank Wycheck, who then threw a lateral pass across the field to Kevin Dyson. The second-year wide receiver scooped up the low throw and sprinted 75 yards untouched down the sideline for the winning touchdown, setting off pandemonium in Nashville. (The Titans eventually reached Super Bowl XXIV, where they lost a 23–16 heartbreaker to the St. Louis Rams.)

By football standards, the Music City Miracle was indeed a marvel. But there is an infinitely greater miracle that takes place far away from the NFL gridiron. It happens inside every true follower of Jesus. It's the moment of spiritual regeneration, when God transforms a dead, sinful heart into one that is alive in Christ. This process is described in Ephesians 2:1–10.

The process of a sinner being saved is nothing short of an extraordinary death-to-life miracle. Consider how scripture describes us pre-salvation:

- "Worthless" (Romans 3:12)
- "Dead in your transgressions and sins" (Ephesians 2:1)
- "By nature deserving of wrath" (Ephesians 2:3)
- "Separate from Christ" (Ephesians 2:12)
- "Without hope and without God in the world" (Ephesians 2:12)
- "Alienated from God" (Colossians 1:21)

The clock was ticking down, and we needed a miracle. Praise be to our loving, merciful God, who miraculously brought us from death to life through Christ!

But because of his great love for us, God, who is rich in mercy,
made us alive with Christ even when we were dead in
transgressions—it is by grace you have been saved.
EPHESIANS 2:4–5

WHERE SAFETY BEGINS

Safety was a concern when the NFL moved the goalposts in 1974. The uprights went from the goal line back to where they were when the league got started—the rear of the end zone. NFL officials hoped players would be less likely to be injured by crashing into an immovable post in the playing area.

The last game with goalposts in the front of the end zone was Super Bowl VIII held at Rice Stadium in Houston. On January 13, 1974, the Miami Dolphins defeated the Minnesota Vikings 24–7 before the uprights migrated off the playing field the following season.

It might seem hard to believe that the NFL could teach us anything of real importance. What might its doctrine be? Maximizing profits? Promoting entertainment? Celebrating pageantry? Actually, the case of the moving uprights can show us how to be safer in our daily lives.

NFL officials determined the goalposts were a potential stumbling block. Their solution was to pluck them out and keep players out of harm's way. There's a lesson in that for each of us, a lesson that Jesus Himself taught: "If your eye causes you to stumble, pluck it out. It is better for you to enter the kingdom of God with one eye than to have two eyes and be thrown into hell" (Mark 9:47).

Jesus wasn't speaking literally. . .but He did call for dramatic action to protect ourselves from sin. Here's an example: How do you interact with your electronic devices? If pornography, or social media gossip, or simply time-wasting web-surfing makes you stumble, Jesus might suggest selling your device, giving it away, or even destroying it.

To paraphrase Jesus' beatitudes, "Blessed are those who do something to protect themselves." Blessed are those who move the goalposts.

> *"Blessed are those who hunger and thirst for righteousness,*
> *for they will be filled."*
> Matthew 5:6

WORK ETHIC

Dallas Cowboy fans can't help but consider running back Emmitt Smith as one of their all-time premier players. After a powerhouse college career with the Florida Gators—a career that included All-American honors, Southeastern Conference MVP, and a spot in the College Football Hall of Fame—Smith was drafted into a Cowboys rebuilding program in 1990. He brought an intense work ethic to Texas.

After fifteen years in the NFL, Smith was inducted into the Pro Football Hall of Fame in 2010. In his acceptance speech, he explained his strategies for career success. "Consistency is necessary for trust, durability, and longevity," Smith said. "You have to show up every week no matter how difficult the game or life might be." But even before that, Smith needed a target. "I wanted to become the all-time leading rusher," he said. "I knew Walter Payton was one of the best to have ever played the game, and I wanted to achieve that level of greatness."

So how did things work out? Smith won rushing titles four times—in 1991, '92, '93, and '95. He contributed to three Dallas Super Bowl victories—after the 1992, '93, and '95 seasons. He had eleven consecutive 1,000-yard seasons, and in 2002 became the NFL's all-time rushing leader, exceeding his hero, Walter Payton. Smith's goal had been realized. All of his hard work had paid off, and his name was in the books. He could truly say, "I've given everything I can possible to the game, on and off the field."

That's a great example for our Christian lives. If we pursue God with the same fervency, we can look forward to the greatest honor of all, His joyful "Well done, good and faithful servant!" (Matthew 25:21).

For we are God's handiwork, created in Christ Jesus to do good works, which God prepared in advance for us to do.
EPHESIANS 2:10

TAKE THAT CATCH AND DO MORE

Accomplishing more than the mere minimum makes a football player—or anyone else—exceptional. It implies extra effort—or extra blessing.

An NFL wide receiver is paid to catch the football. Oftentimes it ends right there. He is tackled immediately or is run out of bounds. But some do more. Some are more than just conquerors of the catch. Some gain more.

Andre Reed was one of those "more" guys. He was known for taking a short pass and turning it into a long gainer. The term "YAC"—Yards After Catch—became his identity. And in 2014 he entered the Hall of Fame.

When Reed retired following the 2000 season, his 951 career receptions ranked third in league history. He was selected to seven Pro Bowls, started in four Super Bowls, and had thirteen seasons of 50-plus catches for the Buffalo Bills. But his gift, according to teammate Steve Tasker, was taking that lesser toss over the middle and turning it into more.

In his Hall of Fame induction speech, Reed recognized Jim Kelly, his quarterback and fellow Hall of Famer, who was there for the festivities, even though he was battling cancer.

"I was known for my toughness going across the middle, making that catch, breaking tackles," Reed said. "But the toughest individual I've ever met in my life is Jim Kelly."

How can you gain a little more ground in life? You can work hard, try hard, and maybe take a little more territory. But it is important to note that human effort has limits. The "more" in your equation belongs to Jesus. He provides the boost that takes you beyond the little catch. The power within that process in life, that burst down the field, is described as being beyond great (see Ephesians 1:19).

It is the gift of God's love in a human being that makes YAC shine.

> *No, in all these things we are more than conquerors*
> *through him who loved us.*
> ROMANS 8:37

RESPONDING TO CONFRONTATION

Urban Meyer was like most other head coaches who spend long hours watching film, reviewing scouting reports, dealing with players' personal problems, and organizing perfect game plans—all the while missing many of their own family functions.

The tension between being a great coach and a great husband and father caused Meyer to quit his head coaching position at Florida—twice. After taking one season off, though, the pull to coaching was still strong, and Meyer accepted the job as head coach at Ohio State. He signed a six-year deal with the university, but not before he agreed to a ten-point contract with his family, written by his daughter Nicki. Here is what Meyer agreed to:

1. My family will always come first.
2. I will take care of myself and maintain good health.
3. I will go on a trip once a year with Nicki—*minimum.*
4. I will not go more than nine hours a day at the office.
5. I will sleep with my cell phone on silent.
6. I will continue to communicate daily with my kids.
7. I will trust God's plan and not be overanxious.
8. I will keep the lake house.
9. I will find a way to watch Nicki and Gigi play volleyball.
10. I will eat three meals a day.

A newspaper story in June 2014 reported that Meyer's daughters say he is indeed putting his family first these days.

Sometimes we need to be told we're headed in the wrong direction. "The Lord sent Nathan to David," 2 Samuel 12:1 says, to confront the king about his adultery with Bathsheba and the killing of her husband, Uriah. It was a painful message, but it changed everything for David.

If God ever sends someone to you, will you listen?

"Repent, then, and turn to God, so that your sins may be wiped out, that times of refreshing may come from the Lord."
Acts 3:19

A PICTURE OF HUMILITY

Let's face it, football fans: a National Football League broadcast isn't the best place in the world to see examples of humility. Sure, many NFL players keep what they do and who they are in perspective, and several of them have stated that they understand that they're able to play at such a high level only because God has given them very special talents and abilities.

But there are also the players—and many of them over the past several years play wide receiver—who seem to enjoy drawing attention to themselves with sometimes crazy end-zone antics more than they enjoy helping their team win.

Arizona Cardinals wide receiver Larry Fitzgerald is different. He never exhibits that "Hey, look at me!" attitude when he makes a big play, and when he scores a touchdown, he first finds the nearest official and hands him the ball—and then celebrates with his teammates.

For Larry, it's about the team first.

But his humble attitude isn't confined to the football field. Those who meet him in non-football settings nearly always come away impressed with his warm smile, firm-but-gentle handshake, and the eye contact he makes with everyone he meets.

The Bible is very clear on this one important point: God loves humility and hates arrogance and pride. When He allows us to accomplish something important, or even great, He is pleased when we celebrate with our "teammates"—our brothers and sisters in Christ—by joining them in giving Him the credit He so richly deserves.

He has shown you, O mortal, what is good. And what does
the LORD require of you? To act justly and to love mercy
and to walk humbly with your God.
MICAH 6:8

LET THE CELEBRATION BEGIN

The 1985 Chicago Bears are undoubtedly one of the greatest teams in NFL history. Led by legendary head coach Mike Ditka and four future Hall of Fame players, the Bears went 15–1, outscored their opponents 456–198, and crushed New England 46–10 in Super Bowl XX.

But it was what happened in early December of that season that truly immortalized this team: the Bears laced up their dancing shoes and filmed the "Super Bowl Shuffle."

It was a huge success. The rap song sold about half a million copies, reached No. 41 on the *Billboard* charts, and quickly entered NFL lore. If you've never seen it before, it's worth a trip to YouTube.

"Sweetness," all-time great running back Walter Payton, kicked things off on the microphone, followed by stars such as quarterback Jim McMahon (wearing a very '80s pair of black shades), linebacker Mike Singletary, defensive end Richard Dent, and defensive lineman William "Refrigerator" Perry. Even little-used Calvin Thomas got airtime with a saxophone solo.

Remarkably (and audaciously), this groundbreaking video was filmed and aired before the team even reached the playoffs. The Bears celebrated their ultimate victory as if it was a certainty.

Christians can do the same. Through Jesus, our spiritual victory has already been won. His death on the cross and glorious resurrection guarantee our eternal triumph over sin, death, and Satan himself.

And we did nothing to earn this victory. "For it is by grace you have been saved, through faith," the apostle Paul wrote, "and this is not from yourselves, it is the gift of God—not by works, so that no one can boast" (Ephesians 2:8–9).

If you're a believer, you can celebrate your victory in Christ every day. The trophy of heaven's eternal glory is yours because of the Savior's amazing love.

> *But thanks be to God! He gives us the victory*
> *through our Lord Jesus Christ.*
> 1 CORINTHIANS 15:57

PEP TALKING

Good football coaches are also excellent motivators.

Part of that motivation is the pep talk—the pregame speech that sends a team into battle, or the halftime session that returns them to the field. The book *Football Nation: Four Hundred Years of America's Game* (Abrams, 2013) shares some colorful examples.

"Gentlemen, you are about to play a game against Harvard," said Tad Jones, a Yale coach of the early twentieth century. "Nothing you do in life will ever again be so important as what you do on the field today."

While coaching Georgia Tech from 1904–19, John W. Heisman—for whom college football's highest honor would be named—added a threat to his talk. "Better to have died as a small boy," he told his players, "than any of you fumble it."

NFL coach Tommy Prothro may have been using reverse psychology when he "motivated" his San Diego Chargers before a 1975 game against Pittsburgh. "If each of you goes out there and plays the best game you'll ever play, if each of you plays over your head, and if each of them plays the worst game they'll ever play," Prothro said, "we still don't have a chance." (San Diego lost 37–0.)

History's most famous pep talk is probably the 1928 "Win One for the Gipper" speech to the Notre Dame team. Summoning the memory of deceased Irish player George Gipp, Knute Rockne turned a 6–0 halftime deficit into a 12–6 victory over previously undefeated Army.

The apostle Paul once gave a pep talk—in written form—to the church at Philippi. But rather than calling his team to "dig deeper" and "give 110 percent," Paul just reminded them where to find the real power to succeed: "I can do all things through Christ which strengtheneth me" (Philippians 4:13 KJV).

Christian success is simply letting Jesus work through you.

Looking unto Jesus the author and finisher of our faith.
HEBREWS 12:2 KJV

JARED ALLEN, DEFENSIVE END

Born April 3, 1982, in Dallas, Texas

Played for Idaho State Bengals (2000–03)

Fourth-round pick in NFL Draft by Kansas City Chiefs (2004)

Played for Chiefs (2004–07), Vikings (2008–13), Bears (2014–2015), Panthers (2015)

First-team All-Pro (2007, '08, '09, '11)

Pro Bowl (2007, '08, '09, '11, '12)

6'6", 255 pounds

"If I don't read my playbook, I'm not successful on the field. My Bible is my playbook for life. If I don't read my Bible, how can I stand firm and wear the full armor of Christ and stand firm against the world if I don't know what's there?"

A WISE MAN

The year was 1970. One of the more inspiring stories ever associated with a forty-three-year-old pro football player was about to be written.

George Blanda was unique. A backup quarterback and a kicker for the Oakland Raiders, his pro experience went back to 1949 with the Chicago Bears. He was a wise leader ready for his moment.

What happened over a five-week span was dizzying. With both his passing and kicking, Blanda led the Raiders to four victories and a tie. And then he retired, right?

No. Blanda kept playing until he was forty-*eight*. His twenty-six seasons stand as the pro football record. When he retired in 1976, he was one month shy of his forty-ninth birthday.

Blanda had cleats in both the NFL and the American Football League. He spent ten years with the Bears, a single game with the Baltimore Colts, and seven seasons with the Houston Oilers. Finally and most notably, he played his last nine years for Oakland.

He finished with 2,002 points and was the NFL's leading career scorer for a time. Most of those points came through his foot, with 335 field goals and 943 PATs. But Blanda also completed 1,911 passes for 26,920 yards and 236 touchdowns. Elected to the Pro Football Hall of Fame in 1981, he died in 2010 at the age of eighty-three.

How do you view aging? Do you respect and appreciate the older people around you? Or are you becoming the older person in your circles? Biblically, aging is a very positive thing. "Moses was eighty years old and Aaron eighty-three when they spoke to Pharaoh," according to Exodus 7:7. Moses served God in strength for another forty years!

Some of the best years of George Blanda's career took place after conventional wisdom said they should have. Don't let advancing age get you down.

> *"Is not wisdom found among the aged?*
> *Does not long life bring understanding?"*
> Job 12:12

NEVER GIVE UP

John Elway had "The Drive," but Buffalo backup quarterback Frank Reich had "The Comeback."

The 1992 AFC Wild Card game between the Bills and the Houston Oilers appeared to be over at halftime as the Oilers led 28–3. To make matters worse, Reich (who was filling in for an injured Jim Kelly) threw an interception early in the third quarter that Bubba McDowell returned for a 58-yard touchdown. Houston then had a 35–3 lead.

But Reich bounced back to lead the Bills on a 50-yard touchdown drive, cutting the deficit to 35–10 midway through the third quarter. An onside kick later, Reich connected on a 38-yard touchdown pass to Don Beebe to make it 35–17. After the Bills forced a punt, Reich tossed a 26-yard scoring pass to Andre Reed, and the margin narrowed to 35–24. A Buffalo interception eventually led to another touchdown and the Bills had trimmed Houston's lead to 35–31.

Amazingly, Buffalo took the lead in the fourth quarter on a 17-yard touchdown pass from Reich to Reed, before Houston tied the game with a field goal. But in overtime, Nate Odomes intercepted Oilers quarterback Warren Moon, setting up Steve Christie's 32-yard field goal to complete the biggest comeback in NFL history.

Oddly, Reich was also at the helm when the Maryland Terrapins recorded the greatest comeback in college football history. Then again, maybe that wasn't so odd. Reich was accustomed to working hard in the shadows. He was a backup at Maryland, behind Boomer Esiason, just like he was a backup in Buffalo to Jim Kelly.

Nobody plans to be a career backup, but preparing well—no matter our circumstances—is the Christian's calling. "Go to the ant," Proverbs 6:6–8 says, "consider its ways and be wise! It has no commander, no overseer or ruler, yet it stores its provisions in summer and gathers its food at harvest." Prepare well, and when your time comes, you'll be ready.

Put your outdoor work in order and get your fields ready;
after that, build your house.
PROVERBS 24:27

WHY WE HAVE RULES

Between 1952 and 1965, Dick "Night Train" Lane was one of the most feared defensive backs in the National Football League. Not only did quarterbacks fear him because of his talent for intercepting the ball (his career 68 picks are the fourth most in NFL history, and his 14 interceptions in 1952, his rookie year, are an NFL record), but receivers and running backs feared him as well because he was such a ferocious tackler.

Lane hit his opponents hard, and he used any means necessary to get them on the ground—including grasping the facemask. The tactic was dangerous, but at the time, it was legal to grasp the facemask of an opposing ball-carrier in an effort to bring him down to the turf.

Recognizing that being dragged down by a facemask put players at risk of serious injury, the NFL finally outlawed the tactic in 1962. Since then, tackling techniques such as "clotheslining," blows to the head with the forearm, and others of Lane's favorite tactics, have been made illegal.

In a very real way, these football rules are much like the "rules" God has given us in His written Word, the Bible. It's easy for some to look at the commandments and prohibitions recorded in the Bible as nothing more than God's way of controlling us and keeping us from enjoying life. But the truth is that He gave us the scriptures so that we can know what pleases Him and what it takes for us to fully enjoy His protections and blessings.

Yes, God has given us some "rules" to follow in our relationship with Him. And when we're careful to follow them, it frees Him to rain down blessings on us.

All Scripture is God-breathed and is useful for teaching, rebuking,
correcting and training in righteousness, so that the servant
of God may be thoroughly equipped for every good work.
2 Timothy 3:16–17

THE COACHING TREE

Tony Dungy made contributions in three seasons as a Pittsburgh Steeler and San Francisco 49er (1977–79), but he'll be remembered far more for his achievements as coach.

Dungy's legacy started as a branch from the "coaching tree" of Steelers chief Chuck Noll. A coaching tree is like a family tree in which a coach defines both his mentors and those he mentored. The Pittsburgh Hall of Famer, who died in 2014, hired Dungy as an NFL assistant coach in 1981. Later, Marty Schottenheimer of Kansas City and Dennis Green of Minnesota were among Dungy's coaching mentors. The coaches Dungy invested in include Lovie Smith and Mike Tomlin. And, of course, there are others.

Dungy was a quiet leader who rarely showed anger on the field. He once said, "The secret to success is good leadership, and good leadership is all about making the lives of your team members or workers better."

Whether with the Tampa Bay Buccaneers or the Indianapolis Colts, Dungy sought to infuse the team's atmosphere with key ingredients for success. In thirteen seasons as an NFL head coach, Dungy had only one sub-.500 record. He won six division championships, a conference championship, and a Super Bowl title. He left a legacy of winning seasons, a sterling reputation, and a group of assistant coaches who have gone on to make their own marks in NFL history.

What Dungy did for coaching in the NFL is similar to what God asks of each of us. Proverbs 1:5 says, "Let the wise listen and add to their learning, and let the discerning get guidance." Dungy was taught by Noll and taught Smith, Tomlin, and others in the same way the apostle Paul was taught by Barnabas and taught Timothy.

The example has always been there. Tony Dungy is just a picture of what it can look like.

The one who receives instruction in the word
should share all good things with their instructor.
GALATIANS 6:6

TRUE TO HIMSELF, HIS GOD, AND HIS WIFE

In a 1975 interview with CBS, now–Hall of Fame Dallas Cowboys quarterback Roger Staubach was asked if living up to his clean-cut, All-American image was a burden. At the time, football fans were well aware of the contrasts in lifestyle between Staubach and New York Jets quarterback Joe Namath, a known womanizer and party animal.

Staubach's answer has become legendary among football fans. He never spoke ill of Broadway Joe, never cast judgment on the New York quarterback's lifestyle. He simply answered, "Everyone in the world compares me to Joe Namath. . .as far as. . .he's single, a bachelor, swinging, and I'm married [with a family]. . .and he's having all the fun. You know, I enjoy sex as much as Joe Namath, only I do it with one girl."

In some corners of our culture, Staubach's answer might have come off as a little square. But to those who value marital fidelity, to those who understand that God created marriage as a lifetime bond between one man and one woman, his words brought smiles and further respect for a true leader who deeply values his relationship with God and with his wife and children (Roger and Marriane Staubach have been married since 1965 and have one son, four daughters, fifteen grandchildren, and one great-grandchild).

Staying true to your God—and to your spouse and children—should never be seen as a burden or as something we "have to do" but as a blessing and a key to true happiness.

The husband should fulfill his marital duty to his wife, and likewise the wife to her husband. The wife does not have authority over her own body but yields it to her husband. In the same way, the husband does not have authority over his own body but yields it to his wife.
1 Corinthians 7:3–4

WHO'S NUMBER ONE?

Pro football steamrolls other sports in popularity.

In a 2014 Harris poll, 35 percent of US sports fans called the NFL their favorite game—a number one result that's held steady since the poll began in 1985. In a distant second, with 14 percent of all fans, was Major League Baseball. . .but throw in the number three sport—college football—and gridiron contests attract 46 percent of all fans.

Though the percentages varied, the rankings mirrored a 2009 ESPN poll. It showed the NFL as the United States' most popular sport with 24.4 percent of those surveyed. Big league baseball was second at 11 percent, while college football took third with 9.5 percent. Baseball had declined since the previous poll in 2003; pro and college football had both gained popularity.

Football fans' hunger for the game is reflected in the massive bids networks make to televise football matchups. In 1965, CBS acquired rights for two years of NFL games for $18.8 million. By 1990, five networks—CBS, ABC, NBC, ESPN, and TNT—were paying $3.6 *billion* to televise four years' worth of games. Of course, the networks intend to earn that money back from advertising—and in the 2014 Super Bowl, a single, thirty-second spot cost a healthy $4 million.

Without a doubt, Americans love their football—and, as the apostle Paul once wrote, God "richly provides us with everything for our enjoyment" (1 Timothy 6:17). But sometimes we can get too much of a good thing, sending our lives out of balance. In the words of Jesus, "No one can serve two masters. Either you will hate the one and love the other, or you will be devoted to the one and despise the other" (Matthew 6:24). In context, Jesus was discussing money—but the principle can apply even to the sports we enjoy.

Don't ever lose sight of the real Number One.

"You shall have no other gods before me."
Exodus 20:3

THE MARK OF PERFECTION

The year 1972 was a tumultuous one, both in America and worldwide.

The Cold War was in full swing and the Vietnam War was still raging. In May that year, Democratic presidential candidate George Wallace was shot five times at a political rally in Maryland. In June, the Watergate scandal broke. And in September, Arab terrorists killed eleven Israeli athletes during the Olympic Games in Munich, Germany.

But for Miami Dolphins fans, everything was just dandy. Don Shula's talented team was on its way to a 17–0 record, capped by a 14–7 win over powerful Washington in Super Bowl VII. To date, it marks the only time in NFL history that a team has won a championship with a perfect season.

Since then, the 2007 New England Patriots have come the closest to matching the feat. Quarterback Tom Brady's bunch became the first team to finish a 16-game regular season undefeated, but they lost a 17–14 shocker to the New York Giants in Super Bowl XLII. The Dolphins' record lived on.

Perfection is hard to come by. In fact, the Bible makes it clear that no one is perfect before God (Romans 3:23). But the remarkable truth of the Gospel is that God will count every true Christian as righteous through faith in His Son, Jesus Christ (Philippians 3:8–9).

This righteousness is given, not earned. Jesus secured our righteousness before a holy God through His atoning work on the Cross. While every Christian still sins, God considers us righteous because He imputes—or credits to our account—the righteousness of Christ.

Jesus took the punishment we deserved on the Cross, while we get His righteousness and all the blessings that come with it. What an amazing deal!

God made him who had no sin to be sin for us, so that in him
we might become the righteousness of God.
2 CORINTHIANS 5:21

LEARNING HOW NOT TO QUIT

Football is like a construction project in some ways. A team's task on game day is to score more points than the other football team, and a certain amount of time is allotted for a certain amount of plays. Once all the plays are completed, there is a victor.

Stanford played California in 1982 and seemed to have a 20–19 victory in hand. Only four seconds were left in the game, and all that remained to finally defeat the Golden Bears was a routine kickoff.

Five laterals later, however, Cal had won. It's known in college football history as "The Play." Its marvels are many, and it can be savored on YouTube.

That improbable tossing of the football from one side of the field to the other, much like a rugby play, can be compared to the building of a wall. Every brick fit. Was it frantic? Sure. But no one can deny that it was one determined effort.

Was there opposition? Yes. The Stanford band was out on the field celebrating. Did it matter? Not in the least. A Cal player scored the winning touchdown, running over a Stanford trombone player in the end zone. The chain of five laterals had covered 57 yards and built a wall known as a 25–20 victory.

When Nehemiah rebuilt the wall of Jerusalem, he never quit working until the last piece was in place. God had given him the time and the energy to finish his task.

Is something in your life tempting you to quit? Do you feel like just taking a knee and heading to the locker room? Maybe it's time for a lateral instead. Just keep The Play moving. Be like the apostle Paul and find a way to get into the end zone (see 2 Timothy 4:7).

Nehemiah won. You can, too.

So the wall was completed on the twenty-fifth of Elul, in fifty-two days.
NEHEMIAH 6:15

A SYMBOL OF REBIRTH

In 2010, five years after Hurricane Katrina wrecked New Orleans, the Saints made their first-ever Super Bowl appearance. From a physical standpoint, the city wasn't even close to full recovery. But a berth in Super Bowl XLIV was a nice distraction, a great story, maybe even part of the healing process.

Led by quarterback Drew Brees, who would be named the game's MVP, the Saints faced Peyton Manning and the Colts. Indianapolis took a 10–6 lead into halftime, but the Saints stunned the Colts by opening the second half with an onside kick. New Orleans' recovery of the kick changed the complexion of the game.

Newark (NJ) Star-Ledger columnist Jerry Izenberg described the impact of the play in a video on the newspaper's website. He said he saw Saints head coach Sean Payton turn to Brees and say, "Okay, we said we'd do it. We did it. You go out there. You play the hand that we dealt you." Izenberg went on, "And Drew Brees did. He started on his 42-yard line and from then on, it was all Saints."

New Orleans outscored the Colts 25–7 in the second half to win the game 31–17. The victory represented the Saints' first, and so far only, Super Bowl title. Another writer for the *Star-Ledger* said the victory would become "a symbol of rebirth for their city."

A new birth is what we experience as we believe in Jesus Christ. We were dead in our sin, beyond any hope. . .until the perfect Lamb of God intervened. Though God had planned it all along, Jesus' death on the Cross was unexpected from a human standpoint. "God demonstrates his own love for us in this," Romans 5:8 says: "While we were still sinners, Christ died for us."

Wherever and whoever you are, rebirth is possible. There is always hope.

So that, having been justified by his grace,
we might become heirs having the hope of eternal life.
Titus 3:7

INTEGRITY

On September 25, 2012, the NFL offices in New York were bombarded with more than seventy thousand phone calls. What was the issue? The integrity of the game.

Less than twenty hours earlier, on the Monday Night Football broadcast, the Seattle Seahawks defeated the Green Bay Packers 14–12 on a play that came to be known as the "Fail Mary." Trailing by five with just seconds to play, Seattle quarterback Russell Wilson launched a 24-yard prayer into the end zone. Although Green Bay defender M. D. Jennings seemingly made a two-handed interception, it was ruled that Seahawks receiver Golden Tate had simultaneous possession. As the clock showed 00:00, Seattle celebrated a come-from-behind victory.

But because replacement officials were involved in the call, many observers called the integrity of the game into question. Fans and sports media alike were concerned that the officials showed two different signals—one raising his arms for a touchdown, the other seemingly indicating an interception—but the hometown team got the call.

Regular NFL officials had been locked out of the game due to a labor dispute. But the "Fail Mary" seemed to prompt the league to bring back its full-time men in stripes to preserve the integrity of the game. They had a new agreement in a matter of days.

Integrity is defined as wholeness. When something is sound or unimpaired, it has integrity. Uprightness, honesty, and sincerity add shades of meaning to the definition.

Far beyond football, integrity is a key element of the Christian life. David prayed, "Declare me innocent, O Lord, for I have acted with integrity; I have trusted in the Lord without wavering" (Psalm 26:1 NLT).

Can we say that everything we do is done with integrity, with uprightness, honesty, and sincerity? We represent a God who is perfectly whole—and who will help us to act with integrity if we ask Him.

The integrity of the upright guides them.
Proverbs 11:3

THE TEAMWORK PARADIGM

In football, we tend to focus on the leaders, game changers, and premier athletes. But sometimes "lesser" players have a more lasting influence.

Brook Berringer was backup to quarterback Tommie Frazier on the Nebraska Cornhusker juggernaut of the mid '90s. He showed up for workouts, didn't complain, stepped onto the field when asked, and returned to the bench when no longer needed. He could have been overlooked—but his personal qualities still commanded attention.

In 1994, as a junior, Berringer started seven games while Frazier dealt with a blood clot. Under Berringer, the Huskers were undefeated, and he became a crowd favorite. Berringer became a symbol of something great, leading his team toward the first of two consecutive national championships.

His senior year? Berringer was back on the bench, playing second fiddle to Frazier.

Nebraska coach Tom Osborne said, "He could have been divisive. He could have led a revolt. He always said the right thing, did the right thing, played his role. [He was] a player who really stood out in my mind representing what team play and teamwork is all about."

In 1996 it looked like Berringer would get a shot at the NFL. But two days before the draft, Berringer, a licensed pilot, died in a crash of his Piper Cub. An entire state mourned. The nation joined in remembering the consummate "team player."

Like Berringer, Christians are called to be team players. The challenges of our "game"—life itself—demand that we help and encourage each other. As the apostle Paul wrote, "God has put the body together, giving greater honor to the parts that lacked it, so that there should be no division in the body, but that its parts should have equal concern for each other" (1 Corinthians 12:24–25).

The best teams always work together.

If one part suffers, every part suffers with it;
if one part is honored, every part rejoices with it.
1 CORINTHIANS 12:26

BUTTER FINGERS?

No football player wants to fumble. . .so how would it feel to be known as the NFL's all-time fumbles leader?

You might be surprised who owns that record: three-time MVP Brett Favre, who quarterbacked Green Bay to a pair of Super Bowl appearances, including a 35–21 victory over the Patriots in 1997.

So what's up with Favre's 166 career fumbles? Or his 336 career interceptions, also an NFL worst? Or the record 525 times he was sacked?

If that makes Favre sound like a butter-fingered, rubber-armed, lead-legged quarterback, there's another side to the coin: He also holds the NFL record for most passes completed, at 6,300—almost 200 more than second-place Peyton Manning. His 71,838 yards gained were a career record until Manning, in the 2015 season, surpassed Favre by 102 yards. Manning also toppled Favre from the top spot of the "career touchdowns thrown" list; as of the beginning of the 2016 season, it reads Manning 539, Favre 508, and Tom Brady and Drew Brees 428. Favre's 23 games with four or more touchdown passes are an NFL best, and he's tied for first for most seasons (four) leading the league in touchdown passes.

What accounts for those records? Beside his football skills, *time.* Favre played twenty seasons in the NFL, racking up 299 consecutive games from 1992 to 2010. With that many games, over that many years, he was bound to accomplish much both positive and negative.

Favre's account parallels the spiritual journey of the apostle Peter. He can be remembered for his failures—looking away from Jesus while walking on water, denying the Lord three times after Jesus' arrest—but that unfairly overlooks Peter's great accomplishments. He was the leader of the twelve disciples, the powerful preacher of Pentecost, the author of two Bible books we still read today. Like Brett Favre, Peter was always "in the game."

How about you? Do you seek the safety of the sidelines, or risk an occasional failure by joining the struggle? Is God calling your number today?

> *"Wherever you hear the sound of the trumpet,*
> *join us there. Our God will fight for us!"*
> Nehemiah 4:20

KNOWING WHAT TO DO...AND WHEN TO DO IT

You don't have to watch a lot of football—at any level—to know that the victory formation (also known as the "genuflect offense" or simply "taking a knee") is a play near the end of the game in which the quarterback takes the snap from center and quickly kneels down, ending the play and keeping the clock winding down.

The victory formation has its origins—or maybe more accurately, its inspiration—in one of the strangest ends to a football game of all time. On November 19, 1978, at Giants Stadium in East Rutherford, New Jersey, what should have been a quick kneel-down by New York Giants quarterback Joe Pisarcik and a New York victory over the Philadelphia Eagles ended in what is now called the "Miracle at the Meadowlands."

The play has been replayed hundreds of times on NFL broadcasts. With his team leading 17–12—and with Philadelphia out of timeouts and only 30 seconds remaining in the game—Pisarcik turned and attempted to hand off to fullback Larry Csonka. But Pisarcik and Csonka botched the handoff, and then Eagles cornerback Herm Edwards scooped up the loose ball and ran it 26 yards into the end zone for a stunning 19–17 Philadelphia victory.

The very next week, teams began using the victory formation at the ends of close games, and teams at all levels of football have been using that tactic ever since—and that because one team seemingly didn't know what to do to close out what should have been a sure win.

You may face situations in which you need to make a decision but aren't sure what you should do. When that happens, there are two directions you can look: at others' past successes and failures. . .or up toward your heavenly Father, who always knows what you should do next.

> . . .from Issachar, men who understood the times
> and knew what Israel should do.
> 1 Chronicles 12:32

THE DIM BECOMES CLEAR

Former University of South Florida offensive lineman Quinterrius Eatmon believes in miracles.

His daughter, Melaynna, was born with septo-optic dysplasia, which means she was born without a corpus callosum—the band of nerve fibers that connects the two halves of the brain—leading doctors to tell Eatmon that his daughter would probably never be able to see. Eatmon's wife, Melyza, said that led to a frantic search for answers.

One day, the then seventeen-month-old reacted to a camera flash, and that was a game-changer. After surgery, Melaynna began making great strides, even beginning to walk. Recently, she has seen objects within six feet and doctors are saying she will probably be able to read large-print books in the future.

"Melaynna is still [classified] legally blind, but you can't tell me she can't see," Eatmon told the *Tampa Tribune*. "When my baby, my angel, my princess looks into my eyes, I feel like I can conquer the world."

When Jesus and His disciples entered Bethsaida, a group of people brought a blind man to Jesus (Mark 8:22–25). Jesus led the man by his hand to the outskirts of the village. When they arrived, Jesus spit on the man's eyes and touched him.

"Do you see anything?" Jesus asked.

"I see people," the man said. "They look like trees walking around."

Jesus touched the man again, completely restoring his sight.

Several Bible commentators point out that the progressive nature of the man's healing serves as an illustration of the way our natural mind is enlightened to spiritual truth. Even after conversion, we start with a dim, murky view of spiritual matters that sharpens over time as we lean in close to Christ.

My goal is that they may be encouraged in heart and united in love,
so that they may have the full riches of complete understanding,
in order that they may know the mystery of God, namely, Christ.
COLOSSIANS 2:2

THE VERY FIRST ONE

Super Bowl XLVIII was played at MetLife Stadium outside New York City on February 2, 2014. Announced attendance was 82,529 and, at the time, the game became the most watched television show in United States history.

The first playoff game in NFL history was played with much less fanfare.

The 1932 season ended with two teams tied for first place—the first time the NFL season had ended with a tie in the standings. It was decided that a playoff game would be played on December 18 to determine the league champion. The Chicago Bears and the Portsmouth Spartans (for the record, Portsmouth is a small town in southern Ohio) played in front of 11,198 fans in Chicago with the Bears winning the game 9–0.

The game was originally scheduled to be played at Wrigley Field (the venerable home of the Chicago Cubs to this day), but a blizzard and subzero wind chill moved the game indoors to Chicago Stadium. The field was reduced to only 80 yards in length and the sidelines were right up against the stands.

The Pro Football Hall of Fame and Museum has a copy of the game program on display in Canton, Ohio. Also of note, the Spartans relocated to Detroit two years later and are still known as the Lions.

In 1933, the NFL divided its teams into two divisions and has played a championship game every year since (now the championship game is called the Super Bowl and is played between the champions of the National Football Conference and the American Football Conference). Over seventy-plus years, the NFL has expanded its playoff system from two teams to twelve, and it seems there is discussion every year to add more teams to the postseason.

Living life as a Christian begins with one simple concept. Romans 10:13 states it clearly: "Everyone who calls on the name of the Lord will be saved." But we Christians are tasked with expanding our knowledge of Christ. Just as the NFL has expanded its postseason, we are to expand our faith.

For this very reason, make every effort to add to your faith goodness; and to goodness, knowledge; and to knowledge, self-control; and to self-control, perseverance; and to perseverance, godliness; and to godliness, mutual affection; and to mutual affection, love.

2 PETER 1:5–7

PHIL DAWSON, KICKER

Born January 23, 1975, in West Palm Beach, Florida

Played for Texas Longhorns (1993–97)

First-team All-American, All-Big 12 (1996, 1997)

Undrafted, picked up by Cleveland Browns (1998)

Played for Browns (1999–2012), 49ers (2013–)

5'11", 200 pounds

"God was in control of everything. He let me go through some experiences to help me make up my mind to follow Him. I'm happy to say years later that the fun in life, the sweet spot in life, is experienced best when it's consistent with the fullness of Christ and His truth."

PLAY UNTIL YOU'RE EXHAUSTED

Football players are taught to give everything they have, otherwise known as "leaving it all out on the field." A snapshot of this actually happening is taken from a 1982 NFL playoff game between the San Diego Chargers and the Miami Dolphins.

On a warm, humid day at the Orange Bowl, Chargers tight end Kellen Winslow Sr. was one among many who, in the words of NBC announcer John Brodie, "played every play as hard as he could." Winslow caught a playoff record thirteen passes for 166 yards. He also blocked a potential game-winning field goal attempt as the Chargers went on to win 41–38 in overtime.

Winslow, a Hall of Fame tight end whose son went on to play the position in the NFL, came into the game with a bruised left shoulder, a strained right rotator cuff, and a sore neck. During the game he suffered cramps in his thigh, both calves, and his lower back. He would play as hard as he could before being helped off, or at times carried off, the field by his teammates.

When it came time to leave the stadium in victory, he moved with no confidence. His body temperature was 105 degrees, and he had lost 13 pounds.

He was exhausted.

Jesus Christ set His face like a flint, as if He were an athlete, to go to the Cross (see Isaiah 50:7). His body had no life. One might say He left it all out on the field of Calvary, only to have God the Father carry Him back to a place where He would be restored.

Rare is the NFL game that transcends life. Winslow said people can't seem to remember who won. That is because the nobler things like leaving it all out on the field and working as hard as you can remain.

Give it your all for God.

Whatever your hand finds to do, do it with all your might.
Ecclesiastes 9:10

DEBT-FREE

Warren Sapp was once one of the most feared players in the NFL.

From 1995 to 2007, the seven-time Pro Bowler and 2013 Hall of Fame inductee wreaked havoc as a 6'2", 300-pound defensive tackle—harassing quarterbacks and clogging running lanes to the tune of 435 tackles, 96.5 sacks, and 19 forced fumbles in thirteen seasons with Tampa Bay and Oakland. For the mayhem he caused, he earned a whopping $82 million over his career.

But in 2012, Sapp filed for bankruptcy, listing his savings account at $826.04. He's not alone. From Lawrence Taylor to Jamal Lewis to Michael Vick, the list of former NFL stars who have gone broke is as long as a Hail Mary from three-time Pro Bowl quarterback Mark Brunell, who, coincidentally, is also on the list. In fact, a staggering 78 percent of former NFL players either declare bankruptcy or experience financial duress within two years of retirement, according to a 2009 *Sports Illustrated* study.

Spiritually speaking, you too were once bankrupt. As today's verse says, you owed God an incalculable debt for your sins. Your liabilities were sky-high, and your assets were zero. From a legal perspective, God had every right to collect on the debt by condemning your soul forever.

Instead, in an amazing act of mercy and love, He offered you the ultimate bailout plan through His Son. Now, by faith in Jesus' atoning work on the Cross, you can live a spiritually rich, debt-free life to the glory and praise of the Savior. It's the solvency plan of a lifetime!

When you were dead in your sins and in the uncircumcision of your
flesh, God made you alive with Christ. He forgave us all our sins,
having canceled the charge of our legal indebtedness, which stood against
us and condemned us; he has taken it away, nailing it to the cross.
COLOSSIANS 2:13–14

OOH, THAT HURTS

Concern over concussions among NFL players is really nothing new. One famous—even infamous—concussion dates back to 1960.

In a November 20 battle between Philadelphia and New York, Eagles linebacker Chuck Bednarik crushed Giants running back Frank Gifford, knocking him out cold. Gifford, the future Hall of Famer, broadcaster, and husband of Kathie Lee, fumbled the football, which was recovered by Philadelphia. The play sealed the Eagles' 17–10 victory and helped propel Philadelphia to the NFL championship.

In a black-and-white photo of the time, Gifford lies flat while Bednarik—the number one draft pick of 1948—celebrates nearby. Gifford spent several days in the hospital with a "deep brain concussion," then skipped the entire 1961 season. Bednarik—also a future Hall of Famer—said his gesture after the play showed joy over the fumble recovery, not the pain he'd inflicted on his opponent.

Fifty years later, Gifford told a reporter that the hit—though devastating—was appropriate. "Chuck hit me exactly the way I would have hit him," he said, "with his shoulder, a clean shot."

By its nature, football is a dangerous game. And though rules have been enacted to limit injuries—such as a prohibition against helmet-to-helmet contact—people still get hurt. That's true in the Christian life, too. Remember these statements of Jesus? "Blessed are those who are persecuted" (Matthew 5:10); "When you are persecuted. . ." (Matthew 10:23); "You will be handed over to be persecuted" (Matthew 24:9); "If they persecuted me, they will persecute you also" (John 15:20).

But whatever harm may come to us, we also have Jesus' promise in John 16:33: "In this world you will have trouble. But take heart! I have overcome the world."

Who is going to harm you if you are eager to do good? But even if you should suffer for what is right, you are blessed. "Do not fear their threats; do not be frightened."
1 Peter 3:13–14

LIVING OUT FORGIVENESS

No one would have blamed Stacey Jackson, the mother of deceased Dallas Cowboys linebacker Jerry Brown Jr., if she felt some anger—even bitterness—toward the man who was driving the car that crashed, killing her son.

That driver, Cowboys defensive tackle Josh Brent, was later convicted of intoxication manslaughter and sentenced to six months in jail for the December 2012 crash that killed Brown. Brent's car was traveling at speeds in excess of 100 miles per hour, and Brent was found to be legally drunk when the crash occurred.

Jackson could have spoken about her personal grief over losing her son, or about how Josh Brent owed her and society a debt. Instead, she spoke about forgiveness, redemption, and second chances: "Josh doesn't have to answer to you or me. He has to answer to God, about what he has done with his second chance," she said to the *Dallas Morning News*. "Who has he helped with this opportunity that he has been given? I [would] have to answer to why I didn't forgive him and live out my life with taking care of my family."

Stacey Jackson demonstrated a rare understanding of the Bible's teaching of forgiveness, an understanding she shared with a man named Stephen, whose story is told in Acts 7. A group of Jewish leaders of that time were none too pleased after Stephen preached the Gospel of Jesus Christ to them, and they reacted with violence. As these men were stoning him to death, Stephen spoke his last words: "Lord, do not hold this sin against them" (verse 60).

Stacey Jackson stands out as an amazing example of this biblical truth: Forgiveness is always better than anger and bitterness. But more than that, it's how God wants us to respond to those who have caused us genuine hurt and anguish.

Be kind and compassionate to one another,
forgiving each other, just as in Christ God forgave you.
EPHESIANS 4:32

MAKE A GOOD TRADE

The date was October 12, 1989. A rare midseason trade changed the course of two NFL franchises. Up north, the Minnesota Vikings, looking to win a championship, acquired a Heisman Trophy winner and All-Pro running back named Herschel Walker. Down south, the 0–5 Dallas Cowboys, with a new owner (Jerry Jones) and a new coach (Jimmy Johnson), were looking to rebuild their team around rookie quarterback Troy Aikman.

The *New York Times* later reported the trade this way: "For Dallas, the trade was seeds planted for the future. For Minnesota, the trade was a bold step in its quest for Super Bowl XXIV on Jan. 28 in the Louisiana Superdome."

The trade did not work out well for the Vikings. The team did not make the Super Bowl, and Walker was released and playing for the Philadelphia Eagles just two and a half years later. The Cowboys continued to wheel and deal with the five players and six draft picks they acquired in the trade, eventually netting future Hall of Fame running back Emmitt Smith and five-time Pro Bowl safety Darren Woodson, among others. The results were impressive: Super Bowl victories following the 1992, 1993, and 1995 seasons.

Just as the Cowboys transformed their roster, the Bible directs the Christian to transform into one who serves Jesus Christ with all his heart, soul, and mind. Paul wrote about the transformation in Romans 12:1–2: "Therefore, I urge you, brothers and sisters, in view of God's mercy, to offer your bodies as a living sacrifice, holy and pleasing to God—this is your true and proper worship. Do not conform to the pattern of this world, but be transformed by the renewing of your mind. Then you will be able to test and approve what God's will is—his good, pleasing and perfect will."

Each Christian has the opportunity to be a champion for Christ by first having the right mind for Christ and then learning how to live for Him.

As a prisoner for the Lord, then, I urge you to live a life
worthy of the calling you have received.
EPHESIANS 4:1

A VIOLENT GAME

William C. Rhoden of the *New York Times* once wrote, "The National Football League markets and manufactures controlled violence and mayhem better than any other league in the history of organized sports."

On the field, pro football still tends to be viewed as positive entertainment. But certain off-the-field incidents, like the one in 2014 involving Baltimore Ravens running back Ray Rice, can tattoo negative images on the NFL body that are hard to remove.

Rice pleaded not guilty to third-degree aggravated assault after allegedly hitting his fiancée in an Atlantic City hotel. Hotel security video caught him dragging her out of an elevator.

Rice was at first suspended for two games and fined three game checks, but when the video went public, the Ravens cut him and the NFL suspended him indefinitely. Rice has apologized to his wife and to all victims of domestic violence, pledging to help all he can.

The idea that disaster is going to hunt down the violent element in the NFL may be new to us. Slowly, and perhaps reluctantly, it is being considered. In the 2010s, concussions became a major topic of discussion. Some retired players have suffered dementia and memory loss. Others have been so traumatized by their football-related injuries that they have taken their own lives. All of these facts fed a lawsuit against the league that was settled for $765 million.

But the sport goes on and is beloved. The concept of "controlled violence and mayhem" that Rhoden wrote about is acceptable and wanted by countless fans.

"The game is appealing and appalling at the same time," wrote Leonard Shapiro of the *Washington Post*. Perhaps we should ask the Judge of the earth to rise up and either redeem it or end it in His own perfect way (see Psalm 94:2).

May slanderers not be established in the land;
may disaster hunt down the violent.
PSALM 140:11

NAME RECOGNITION

Back in 1933, as America was still in the throes of the Great Depression, NFL owner George Preston Marshall changed his team's name from the Boston Braves to the Boston Redskins. Eighty years later, current Washington Redskins owner Daniel Snyder found himself caught in a nationwide firestorm over the appropriateness of a nickname that many people denounced as racially insensitive to Native Americans.

From newspaper columns to the White House, everyone with public platforms began voicing their opinions about "Redskins." Many called for the team to change its name immediately. Others, including team officials, maintained that the name honored the nation's indigenous peoples.

Few sports team names have ever caused more controversy. But there is a name that has generated far more discussion worldwide for the past two thousand years. It's the most important name in history: Jesus Christ.

Because of who He is (the eternal Son of God) and what He has done (purchased salvation for us through His death and resurrection), Jesus bears "the name that is above every name." No name is greater, more powerful, or more worthy of praise in the universe.

One day, the mere mention of Jesus' name will cause all creation—both the wicked and the righteous—to fall on their knees and give Him the glory He deserves. For the wicked, this will be a terrifying day of judgment. For the righteous, this will be a marvelous day as they bask in the glory and majesty of their Savior.

Don't wait until it's too late. Worship Jesus' name today!

Therefore God exalted him to the highest place and gave him the name that is above every name, that at the name of Jesus every knee should bow, in heaven and on earth and under the earth, and every tongue acknowledge that Jesus Christ is Lord, to the glory of God the Father.
PHILIPPIANS 2:9–11

A CHANGE IN THE RULES?

We've all seen key plays replayed in slow motion, from multiple angles. Defenders lunge in an attempt to get to the quarterback. The thrower releases, then winces as helmets, elbows, knees, and shoulders conspire to punish him.

It's amazing that anyone can survive such punishment. Many times, the quarterback shakes off the blows and returns to the huddle. Occasionally, a hush falls over the crowd as he's assessed for injuries. Whether he's helped off the field or leaves under his own power, we admire the grit that makes a player risk it all for the game he loves.

There was a time when contact between defenders and quarterbacks was common. But one notable hit changed the course of quarterback protection.

In 2008, the New England Patriots were at the top of their game, coming off a perfect 16–0 regular season in '07. In the first quarter of their first game, Chiefs safety Bernard Pollard, fighting to sack the quarterback, got his helmet into Tom Brady's knee. Brady had to leave the game and ultimately missed the entire season.

While the hit was legal, it did cause the NFL to consider greater protections for quarterbacks. By 2009 new rules were in place; today, similar hits usually receive a penalty on the field and sometimes a fine from the league office. Change is often necessary and good.

God, though, never needs to change His rules. They're as applicable today as when they were first spoken and written. As Jesus said, "Heaven and earth will pass away, but my words will never pass away" (Matthew 24:35).

No revisions, additions, or deletions are ever called for. God thought of everything.

"Every word of God is flawless; he is a shield to those who take refuge in him. Do not add to his words, or he will rebuke you and prove you a liar."
PROVERBS 30:5–6

THE POWER OF A PROMISE

On October 3, 2009, eight American soldiers were killed and twenty-two were wounded during a battle with nearly three hundred Taliban insurgents near Kamdesh, Afghanistan. Daniel Rodriguez was shot in the leg, neck, and shoulder. His friend, PFC Kevin Thompson, was among the dead.

Two weeks prior to the attack, the two men had made a pledge to one another—to follow their hearts and to do what they wanted to do if they made it home. For Rodriguez, that included getting a college degree and playing college football. The combat veteran, who had been playing football since his Pee Wee days and then went on to letter in high school, had every intention of keeping his promise.

So the Purple Heart and Bronze Star recipient put together a video to showcase his talents. The footage included his workouts, his high school playing days, and combat footage. His plan worked. Clemson head coach Dabo Swinney saw the video and offered him a spot on the team as a walk-on.

Rodriguez played mostly on special teams. And on Military Appreciation Day, he led the charge with the American flag, which seems fitting as he honored those who fell in the line of duty.

On the day of Pentecost, the apostle Peter preached a sermon in which he spoke about a different sort of promise that was also fulfilled: "Repent and be baptized, every one of you, in the name of Jesus Christ for the forgiveness of your sins. And you will receive the gift of the Holy Spirit. The promise is for you and your children and for all who are far off—for all whom the Lord our God will call" (Acts 2:38–39).

Paul, a servant of Christ Jesus, called to be an apostle and set apart for the gospel of God—the gospel he promised beforehand through his prophets in the Holy Scriptures regarding his Son.
ROMANS 1:1–3

THREE-PEAT

Even the greatest football teams find it hard to three-peat.

Through the 2015 season, seventeen teams had won consecutive league championships, either in the NFL or the old American Football League: the 1922–23 Canton Bulldogs; the 1932–33 and 1940–41 Bears; the 1948–49 Eagles; the 1952–53 Lions; the 1954–55 Browns; the 1958–59 Colts; the 1960–61 Oilers; the 1961–62 Packers; the 1964–65 Bills; the 1972–73 Dolphins; the 1974–75 and 1978–79 Steelers; the 1988–89 49ers; the 1992–93 Cowboys; the 1997–98 Broncos; and the 2003–04 Patriots.

But only two teams have ever won *three* straight titles, and both were from Green Bay—the 1965–67 Packers, who claimed the first two Super Bowl titles, and, a generation earlier, the 1929–31 squad. (The 1932 Packers almost earned a "four-peat" but for an oddity in the NFL rankings of the day: Their 10–3–1 record was four wins better than the 6–1–6 result of the Chicago Bears and the 6–1–4 tally of the Portsmouth Spartans, later to become the Detroit Lions. But since ties didn't count at all in the win percentages, Green Bay's three losses kept them out of title contention.)

If a team wins three straight league championships, you'll pay attention. Don't you think you should take note if Jesus says something three times?

In His Sermon on the Mount, Jesus urged His followers to do good—to give to the poor, to pray, and to fast—without drawing attention to themselves. Each time, Jesus commented that God, "who sees what is done in secret, will reward you" (Matthew 6:4, 6, 18).

One word from Jesus should be plenty for us. A repeated word carries even greater emphasis. But a three-peat? Pay attention!

> *"Heaven and earth will pass away,*
> *but my words will never pass away."*
> MARK 13:31

AN IMPRACTICAL DECISION

One of the rarer stories in football features a player rejecting the prevailing utilitarianism of American culture.

Utilitarianism is when you choose usefulness or practicality over beauty or aesthetic value. In football it is simple—you always take the money. You've got to get paid.

Even Christian athletes need to earn a living. The argument goes that you always take the money to "build your platform" and "provide for your family" for "the greater good" to bless "the greatest number of people."

Alternatives that would involve considering the captivating beauty of God or devoting one's twenties to a process of Christian discipleship apart from football are not seriously considered.

Enter Chris Norman. In 2012, the Michigan State University linebacker chose seminary over the NFL. He was paid not in money, but by the reward an ancient psalm writer enjoyed: "One thing I ask from the Lord, this only do I seek: that I may dwell in the house of the Lord all the days of my life, to gaze on the beauty of the Lord and to seek him in his temple" (Psalm 27:4).

"In the Gospel there's a story about somebody that stumbles across a field and then they found a treasure hidden in that field," Norman said. "As a result of finding that treasure, they sold everything they had so they can buy that field. That's pretty much what happened to me when I found Christ. So once I met Him and fell absolutely in love with Him, everything else was not as attractive in comparison."

Norman was influenced by the words of author John Piper, who writes in *Don't Waste Your Life* that every waking moment should be lived to the glory of God. Or, as Norman said it another way: "It's my pleasure to live for His glory."

Not to us, Lord, not to us but to your name be the glory,
because of your love and faithfulness.
Psalm 115:1

"HE COULD HAVE PLAYED EVERY POSITION"

You might envision a player named "Bronko Nagurski" as a tough guy. You'd be right.

Bronko wasn't really his first name. He got the moniker when a teacher mispronounced the name Bronislaw. "Bronko" stuck—and well represented his future football style.

It seemed that Nagurski could smash through any line, offensive or defensive. During his college career at Minnesota, he gained All-American honors on both sides of the ball—and continued his two-way play with the Chicago Bears. Bronko could even pass; in the NFL's first official championship game in 1933, he threw for two touchdowns, including the game winner.

Legendary Notre Dame coach Knute Rockne said, "Nagurski is the only football player I ever saw who could have played every position." In 1937, after eight NFL seasons, Nagurski left the Bears for another role: professional wrestler. His crushing style earned a pair of world titles, but in 1943, when the Bears called him out of retirement, Nagurski agreed.

His bonus season featured the same no-holds-barred play. When Chicago needed him most, the thirty-five-year-old delivered on plays that led to another championship. It's no surprise that Bronko was part of the first Hall of Fame class in 1963.

The apostle Paul would have enjoyed Nagurski's all-encompassing game. The great missionary described his own style similarly: "To the Jews I became like a Jew, to win the Jews. To those under the law I became like one under the law. . . . To those not having the law I became like one not having the law. . . . To the weak I became weak, to win the weak. I have become all things to all people so that by all possible means I might save some" (1 Corinthians 9:20–22).

Paul "played every position" for the Gospel. So can we.

"As for you, be strong and do not give up,
for your work will be rewarded."
2 CHRONICLES 15:7

THE WAY OF WEAKNESS

One way to win a Super Bowl is to have your Hall of Fame quarterback throw for 300 yards.

And then there is the way of weakness.

In 2001, the Baltimore Ravens won the Super Bowl with defense, a running game, and a quarterback, in that order. Over four playoff games, quarterback Trent Dilfer did just enough to win—meaning he threw only one interception. His Super Bowl line was weak—12 of 25 passing, 153 yards, one touchdown. But history records that weakness won, 34–7, over the New York Giants.

Dilfer lasted thirteen years in the NFL, throwing 129 interceptions to 113 touchdowns. He had just one year with Baltimore—his championship season—and played for five other teams. It's interesting that Dilfer owns a Super Bowl ring while Miami Dolphins Hall of Famer Dan Marino does not.

Weakness isn't all bad. Dilfer realized that he belonged to a strong community and didn't try to accomplish everything himself. The Ravens defense, which allowed an average of 10.3 points per game that season, needed only a handful of excellent plays from the offense to win games.

God isn't surprised or offended by human weakness. He often uses it in His plan. The apostle Paul well understood how God works and told the Corinthians, "If I must boast, I will boast of the things that show my weakness" (2 Corinthians 11:30).

A "weak" Christian realizes that he belongs to Christ. When we surrender our dreams of power and glory, we are rescued and redeemed, able to walk according to the Holy Spirit (see Romans 8:1–4). Our victories can then be appreciated as gifts.

The way of weakness is the way to God.

He gives strength to the weary
and increases the power of the weak.
ISAIAH 40:29

"ORDINARY STEPS IN THE RIGHT DIRECTION"

Ever wondered where the phrase "quarterback sack" came from? Look to the premier defensive end of the 1960s, David "Deacon" Jones.

"I did come up with the term *sack* to describe the devastation I was bringing on the poor, cringing quarterbacks in the NFL," Jones said. "I thought it was lots better than saying, 'Jones tackles the QB behind the line for another loss of yardage.' . . . It had a ring to it, and it caught on with the sportswriters. But I tell you, doing it was a lot more fun than talking about it."

Jones was always one to speak his mind. Whiners were a favorite target: "You think society is to blame for the mess you made of yourself?" he asked. More positively, Jones said, "It took me a long time to figure out that real big-time success comes from taking lots of small, ordinary steps in the right direction. And you can't ever take the next step until you take the first."

Jones's quarterback-terrifying steps led to his being named to the Pro Bowl eight times. After a fourteen-year career with the Rams, Chargers, and Redskins, he was inducted into the Hall of Fame in 1980 in his first year of eligibility. Ultimately, Jones was named to the 1960s All-Decade Team and the All-Time NFL Team in 2000.

Known as the "Secretary of Defense," Jones knew his role and played it with everything he had. His philosophy and career are reminiscent of our spiritual walk as described in 1 Corinthians 15:58: "Stand firm. Let nothing move you. Always give yourselves fully to the work of the Lord, because you know that your labor in the Lord is not in vain."

Giving ourselves to God's work is what transforms us from spectators to participants, from ineffective to powerful. Be bold. Take that first step. Then take another.

"If you love me, keep my commands."
John 14:15

SCOUT TEAMS

We football fans don't have a chance to see all the hours of preparation it takes for our favorite college football teams to be ready to play on Saturday afternoons. And we certainly don't get a chance to see the role that scout teams play in making their programs successful.

Scout teams are made up mostly of walk-ons (players who join college teams without the benefit of an athletic scholarship) and redshirt freshman (scholarship players who aren't yet ready to play). Their job is to help the team prepare for the upcoming game by emulating, as best they can, what the next opponent likes to do.

Scout team players do all the same work as the first-line players, but without receiving any of the recognition. Their on-field exploits are limited to practices during the week, and they don't usually suit up for games or travel with the team for away games.

For a season anyway, scout team players are "nobodies"—at least as far as the fans and media are concerned. Yet most coaches and players will tell you that scout teams are absolutely essential to the success of a football program. Without them, they would say, it would be impossible to prepare for games by engaging in live game action during practice.

The Bible has a lot to say about being prepared for acts of service, and it includes some examples of people God used to prepare others to change the world for Jesus Christ (Barnabas and Aquila and Priscila in the book of Acts, for example).

Is God calling you to be something of a "lesser light"—someone who works behind the scenes to prepare others to serve Him? If so, then you should feel blessed to be part of His own "scout team."

So Christ himself gave the apostles, the prophets, the evangelists, the pastors and teachers, to equip his people for works of service, so that the body of Christ may be built up.
Ephesians 4:11–12

GREG SCHIANO, COACH

Born June 1, 1966, in Wyckoff, New Jersey

Played for Bucknell Bison (1984–87)

Penn State Nittany Lions defensive backs coach (1991–95)

Chicago Bears defensive assistant (1996–97)

Chicago Bears defensive backs coach (1998)

Miami Hurricanes defensive coordinator (1999–2000)

Rutgers Scarlet Knights head coach (2001–2011)

Tampa Bay Buccaneers head coach (2012–2013)

Ohio State defensive coordinator and associate head coach (2016 –)

 "Just Pray. Just Pray."

BAD FADS

The 2012 NFL season was the year of the Griffin. . .and Wilson. . .and Kaepernick.

That season, three young, dual-threat quarterbacks took the league by storm. Robert Griffin III won the league's Rookie of the Year Award and led the Washington Redskins to their first division title since 1999. Russell Wilson guided Seattle to the second round of the playoffs, and Colin Kaepernick propelled San Francisco to Super Bowl XLVII.

But it wasn't just this playmaking trio's precocious skills that made headlines. Interestingly, all three enjoyed great success running the read-option offense. The NFL has always featured running quarterbacks (see: Cunningham, Randall; Tarkenton, Fran; Vick, Michael; etc.), but these three quarterbacks in particular popularized a growing offensive trend in the league.

The NFL is a cyclical game of fads. If it's not the read-option, it's the West Coast offense, no-huddle, spread, or wildcat. Who knows? Maybe the single-wing will reappear one day.

Fads might work in the NFL, but not in the Christian faith. God is unchanging, and so is His inspired, inerrant Word. Christians must be careful not to get caught up in supposedly new spiritual ideas or revelations.

As the apostle Paul says in today's passage, we are to "hold firmly" to the true Gospel—"that Christ died for our sins according to the Scriptures, that he was buried, [and] that he was raised on the third day according to the Scriptures" (1 Corinthians 15:3–4).

That's the beauty of the Gospel of Jesus Christ. It doesn't need to be added to or improved upon. It's perfect the way God revealed it to us in Holy Scripture.

Now, brothers and sisters, I want to remind you of the gospel I preached
to you, which you received and on which you have taken your stand.
By this gospel you are saved, if you hold firmly to the word
I preached to you. Otherwise, you have believed in vain.
1 CORINTHIANS 15:1–2

RULE BREAKERS

Not every NFL record is one you'd *want* to hold.

The league tracks many records, for both individuals and teams, and among the latter are several related to penalties. Most penalties in a game? Twenty-six, by the 2014 Chicago Bears and the 2015 Dallas Cowboys. Most penalties in a season? That's 163, by the 2011 Raiders—while the 2013 Seattle Seahawks claim the most yards penalized in a season with 1,415. The most penalty yards in a game is 212, by the 1999 Titans.

Then you have records like "Most Consecutive Seasons Leading League, Most Penalties" and "Most Consecutive Seasons Leading League, Most Yards Penalized." The 1941–44 Bears hold the mark for the former, while the same team (plus its 1939–40 editions) extends the record for the latter.

You might think all those penalties would hurt a team's chances, but with the World War II–era Bears, you'd be wrong. In the six straight seasons they led the league in penalty yards, Chicago won its division four times, and the NFL championship three times. They never finished worse than second; never had a win percentage of less than .667. It seems unfair that rule-breakers would be so successful.

Ever felt that way about people you see, whether coworkers, entertainers, politicians. . .even pro athletes? If so, you'd be like the prophet Jeremiah, who asked God, "Why does the way of the wicked prosper? Why do all the faithless live at ease?" (Jeremiah 12:1). A psalm writer also struggled with the apparent prosperity of the arrogant and sinful: "This is what the wicked are like—always free of care, they go on amassing wealth" (Psalm 73:12).

But don't think those complaints are the whole story—for God's perspective, read all of Jeremiah 12 and Psalm 73.

When I tried to understand all this, it troubled me deeply till I entered
the sanctuary of God; then I understood their final destiny.
Psalm 73:16–17

SOBER JUDGMENT

Denied the chance to play on his high school team, Steve Van Buren dropped out and worked in a foundry. Two years later, he returned to school and made the team. Then he won a scholarship to LSU.

College teammates called him "Wham-Bam," a reference to the way he ran and hit. The number one draft pick of 1944 by Philadelphia, Van Buren would lead the Eagles to three straight division titles and two league championships. In the 1948 title game against the Chicago Cardinals, Van Buren would make the lone score on a day when more than seven inches of snow fell. He led the NFL in rushing four times, surpassing 1,000 yards twice. Van Buren retired in 1952 as the NFL's career rushing leader.

"I've seen them all—Jim Thorpe, Red Grange, Bronko Nagurski," said "Greasy" Neale, Van Buren's coach, "but he's the greatest." Andy Reid, Eagles coach from 1999 to 2012, said Van Buren "was special in person, too, humble about his own accomplishments and encouraging to others."

After being drafted, Van Buren waited three weeks to sign his contract, saying later he wasn't sure he was good enough for the NFL. When asked what he thought his greatest accomplishments were, he replied, "None." In his Hall of Fame induction comments he said, "Since you people can't hear too good and I'm not too good a speaker, I won't say much." That sentence represents about a third of his entire speech.

The apostle Paul might well have approved of Van Buren's self-effacing style. "Do not think of yourself more highly than you ought," Paul wrote in Romans 12:3, "but rather think of yourself with sober judgment, in accordance with the faith God has distributed to each of you."

We don't have to promote ourselves. Remember that God knows the good we do.

Let someone else praise you, and not your own mouth;
an outsider, and not your own lips.
PROVERBS 27:2

TOUCHDOWN FAIL

Because he competed in 282 straight games, Minnesota Vikings defensive end Jim Marshall was nicknamed "Ironman." But he's just as famous for a blunder he committed in an October 25, 1964, game against the San Francisco 49ers.

San Francisco quarterback George Mira dropped back, scrambled to avoid the rush, then noticed a wide-open Billy Kilmer, who was playing halfback at the time—later in his career, he would play quarterback for Washington. Mira hit Kilmer in the flat, and Kilmer did everything he could to break through three Minnesota defenders, twisting and turning and fighting for every yard, before losing the ball. That's when Marshall entered the picture. Scooping up the loose ball, he sprinted toward the end zone—his own end zone.

At least one of Marshall's teammates chased him, trying to tell him to turn around, but he was unable to get close enough. Marshall ended up running 66 yards for what turned out to be a 49ers safety.

"My first inkling that something was wrong," Marshall said after the game, "was when a 49er player gave me a hug in the end zone."

At least he had a sense of humor about it.

In the middle of battle, it's easy to become disoriented. After the Last Supper, Jesus' twelve disciples got into a dispute about which of them was the greatest. It was a silly argument, completely inappropriate for God's people. But Jesus gently corrected them, then said, "Satan has asked to sift all of you as wheat. But I have prayed for you, Simon, that your faith may not fail. And when you have turned back, strengthen your brothers" (Luke 22:31–32).

From time to time, we'll all lose our bearings and get on the wrong path. But as long as we have breath, it's never too late for us to change direction.

But whenever anyone turns to the Lord, the veil is taken away.
2 Corinthians 3:16

LIVING ON A PRAYER

The NFL is by no means a religious institution, but any given football Sunday is typically filled with prayer. Players present petitions in the pregame locker room and make divine appeals on the sidelines. End zone–bound ball-carriers point skyward. White-knuckled fans offer fourth-quarter supplications. And spiritually like-minded opponents prayerfully congregate postgame at midfield.

Are the motives behind all these prayers pure? Well, that's a topic for another day. Suffice it to say that an NFL game includes a lot of heavenward requests.

Here's what's clear: prayer should be constant in every Christian's life. In addition to today's short-but-sweet verse, consider the following scripture passages exhorting believers to pray:

- "Devote yourselves to prayer, being watchful and thankful" (Colossians 4:2).
- "And pray in the Spirit on all occasions with all kinds of prayers and requests" (Ephesians 6:18).
- "Do not be anxious about anything, but in every situation, by prayer and petition, with thanksgiving, present your requests to God" (Philippians 4:6).

Prayer should never be viewed as a burden, but instead as a wonderful blessing. It's a way that sinful, finite humans can actually communicate with the holy and eternal Lord God Almighty. He loves to hear from His children and bless prayers offered in humble faith (Mark 11:24).

Remember, too, that prayers are for your benefit, not God's. When you pray, you're not telling the omniscient, sovereign God of the universe anything He doesn't already know. Prayer is about humbling yourself before the Lord and acknowledging your need for Him in worship, gratitude, and petitions.

Not sure how to pray? Check out the "Lord's Prayer"—Jesus' helpful model in Matthew 6:5–15. But most importantly, get on your knees and cry out to your Lord and Savior—today and every day!

Pray continually.
1 THESSALONIANS 5:17

THE TOUCHDOWN DANCE

One of the gifts professional football has given mankind is the touchdown dance. Out of the world of entertainment has come a reminder that dancing in its purest form is pleasing to God.

Elmo Wright is said to be the inventor of the touchdown dance. On a play when he was playing for the University of Houston, he spontaneously high-stepped to avoid a tackle, which led to his high-stepping right into the end zone. He kept on doing it with the NFL's Kansas City Chiefs, laying a cornerstone for a temple of dancing in NFL end zones.

Many NFL players have danced over the years. A sure progression from the 1970s, 1980s, and 1990s can be traced through the lives of three pros who proved to be dancers. Let us examine the dancing trendsetting of Billy "White Shoes" Johnson, Ickey Woods, and Deion Sanders.

Johnson, a wide receiver for the Houston Oilers, did the "Funky Chicken." Woods, a running back for the Cincinnati Bengals, did the "Ickey Shuffle" (three steps to the left, three steps to the right. . .). Sanders, a Hall of Fame cornerback/return man who is recognized as perhaps the greatest of all time, did the "Prime Time Dance." Later came Sundays filled with countless creative displays in the 2000s and 2010s.

God enjoys dancing (Psalm 30:11). There is a time for it (Ecclesiastes 3:4). It might be when mourning is ready to be replaced.

A touchdown can do it. And a dance can be a form of obedience before a holy God, who is the inventor of happiness. You can do a happy dance before Him (2 Samuel 6:14). Dance. Catch that truth and own it.

Thy kingdom come, Thy will be done on earth as it is in heaven. . .when it comes to the purification of professional football dancing.

Let them praise his name with dancing.
PSALM 149:3

AMAZING FAITH. . .AND WORK ETHIC

When one University of Arkansas assistant football coach sat in a living room with the family of Brandon Burlsworth, a high school football player living in Harrison, Arkansas, he wasn't about to make Brandon a bunch of promises about playing time—or even a scholarship.

Brandon was a big boy—probably over 300 pounds at the time—and he was a good high school player. But the UA coaching staff didn't believe he could amount to anything as an NCAA-level player, so they declined to offer him a scholarship.

What these coaches couldn't see was the kid's huge heart, old-school work ethic. . .and faith.

The Razorback coaches invited Brandon to come to the University of Arkansas—on his family's dime—and try out for the team as a walk-on. Brandon certainly made the most of the opportunity. He amazed his coaches and teammates with his hard work and dedication, and he was soon granted a scholarship.

But that wasn't the end of it. Brandon earned All-Southeastern Conference honors as an offensive guard in 1997 and 1998 and was named first-team All-American his senior year. Then, in April of 1999, the Indianapolis Colts drafted him in the third round of the NFL Draft.

Sadly, Brandon died in a car accident ten days after the draft. After his death, Arkansas coach Houston Nutt started a saying that is still popular at UA: "Do it the Burls Way," meaning doing things the right way—through hard work and dedication—even when no one is watching.

Have you ever felt like God is calling you to something you don't feel talented or gifted enough to accomplish? If you have, then it may just be a matter of dedicating yourself, working harder. . .and trusting Him to do it through you.

A sluggard's appetite is never filled,
but the desires of the diligent are fully satisfied.
PROVERBS 13:4

IDENTITY CRISIS?

In 1950, the American press named Jim Thorpe the most outstanding athlete of the twentieth century to that point. He was, after all, a man who successfully competed in football, baseball, and the Olympics.

But athletic achievements and fame didn't make life easy. Thorpe faced many struggles. He was an "Indian" in an era when Native Americans were just gaining citizenship. His Olympic gold medals (for the pentathlon and decathlon) were later taken away because he'd earlier played semi-pro baseball, violating the Olympics' rules for amateurism. Through it all, Thorpe's inner drive seemed all-consuming.

One of Thorpe's Olympic teammates, Abel Kiviat, said, "There wasn't anything he couldn't do. All he had to see is someone doing something and he tried it. . .and he'd do it better."

Thorpe's NFL career—with the Canton Bulldogs, Oorang Indians, Rock Island Independents, New York Giants, and Chicago Cardinals—landed him in the first class of the Pro Football Hall of Fame. He played from 1920 through 1928 as a tailback, fullback, and kicker.

Thorpe's identity was sports. During the 1912 Olympics in Sweden, King Gustav V told Thorpe, "Sir, you are the greatest athlete in the world." His life was tied to the games he loved.

As Christians, our identity comes from the Lord we follow. "If anyone is in Christ," the apostle Paul wrote, "the new creation has come: The old has gone, the new is here!" (2 Corinthians 5:17).

Whether we're talented athletes, successful business leaders, bestselling writers—or simply "average Joes"—we are first and foremost children of God. All we do should be for His honor.

You were taught, with regard to your former way of life, to put off your old self, which is being corrupted by its deceitful desires; to be made new in the attitude of your minds; and to put on the new self, created to be like God in true righteousness and holiness.
EPHESIANS 4:22–24

THE GOSPEL ERASES DIVIDING LINES

Former Georgia wide receiver Malcolm Mitchell wasn't satisfied with his reading level when he entered college, so he decided to work as hard at improving his reading skills as he did at his football skills. Books became his constant companion, and eventually he worked his way through the *Hunger Games* series in two days.

One day, while visiting a Barnes & Noble, a customer named Kathy Rackley began chatting with him. She was excited about the book club she had just joined and had to tell a fellow bibliophile. She had no idea who Mitchell was at the time. He asked her if he could join her book club.

"I don't know if you want to join mine," she said. "We're all forty-, fifty-, and sixty-year-old women.' "

That didn't bother Mitchell in the least, so he became the only male member of an otherwise all-female book club. He was also the youngest by a generation, and the only African-American in the group. But none of those things mattered to him. He had found a group of people who shared his passion for the written word, and that was the tie that bound them.

Something similar takes place anytime a sinner is grafted into the family of God. All natural and worldly dividing lines vanish, just as Paul wrote to the Galatian church (3:28): "There is neither Jew nor Gentile, neither slave nor free, nor is there male and female, for you are all one in Christ Jesus."

Therefore, "Come out from them and be separate, says the Lord.
Touch no unclean thing, and I will receive you." And, "I will be
a Father to you, and you will be my sons and daughters,
says the Lord Almighty."
2 CORINTHIANS 6:17–18

COURAGE IN THE FACE OF PERSECUTION

Kenny Washington isn't as well known as Jackie Robinson, but the two have a lot in common. Around the same time Robinson broke through the long-standing "color barrier" in Major League Baseball, Washington was doing the same in professional football.

As a collegiate athlete at UCLA, Washington faced racial discrimination and taunts, but that didn't stop him from starring in football and baseball. The discrimination didn't stop after Washington graduated college, either. He was obviously one of the best players in the nation, but at the time the National Football League did not welcome black players onto its teams.

Washington spent several years playing in semi-pro football leagues in California before the NFL lifted its ban on African-American players and allowed him to sign with the Los Angeles Rams. By the time Washington signed with the Rams in 1946, he was a twenty-eight-year-old running back with bad knees, but he still averaged a very respectable 6.1 yards per carry over his three seasons in the NFL (1946–1948).

Like Robinson, Washington faced racial slurs but also dirty play on the part of tacklers. But he courageously endured the persecution and helped pave the way for thousands of African-American players who have since played in the NFL.

Persecution is never fun to endure, but the Bible promises believers that they will face it—and in many different ways. But God's Word also promises that we can overcome by remembering that when we suffer for Christ, we can be reminded of the future joy we will experience in God's eternal kingdom.

Dear friends, do not be surprised at the fiery ordeal that has come on you to test you, as though something strange were happening to you. But rejoice inasmuch as you participate in the sufferings of Christ, so that you may be overjoyed when his glory is revealed.
1 PETER 4:12–13

FAMILY TRADITION

Archie Manning was a highly regarded college quarterback and the second overall pick in the 1971 NFL Draft. But playing most of his pro career with a dismal New Orleans Saints team, he never appeared in a Super Bowl or even made it to the postseason. Manning's record—35 wins, 101 losses, and 3 ties—is the worst in history for a player with more than 100 starts. Ironically, Archie is the father of the extraordinarily successful quarterbacks Peyton and Eli Manning.

Peyton's Tennessee Volunteers were the 1997 SEC champions, and he became the number one draft pick of 1998. By 2006, Peyton had been named the league's MVP twice and led the Colts to a Super Bowl victory. More MVP awards followed, in 2008 and 2009. After missing all of 2011 due to surgery, Peyton signed a deal with Denver and promptly earned the NFL Comeback Player of the Year Award. In his second year with the Broncos, he earned a fifth MVP award and led his team to the Super Bowl against the Seattle Seahawks. His third and final year earned him another ring.

Eli Manning, Archie's youngest son, was the number one draft pick of 2004. His start as a quarterback was rocky, but he led his New York Giants to Super Bowl wins after the 2007 and 2011 seasons, winning MVP honors each time.

Sons tend to look up to their fathers. But with the Mannings, the father also looks up to his sons. After they'd found the success that eluded him, Archie said, "I never got to do it, so I'm very excited for them."

In families, there's no place for jealousy. The body of Christ is certainly a family, too. We are, as the apostle Paul said, to "rejoice with those who rejoice." And, he added, to "mourn with those who mourn" (Romans 12:15).

That's a family tradition worth holding on to.

Be devoted to one another in love.
Honor one another above yourselves.
ROMANS 12:10

AGAINST THE ODDS

Anyone watching Monday Night Football on January 3, 1983, remembers this play.

In the fourth quarter, the Minnesota Vikings were leading the Dallas Cowboys 24–13. The Cowboys were backed up to their own one-yard line. They planned to hand the ball to fullback Ron Springs, have him pick up a couple of yards, and then punt.

But Springs misunderstood the play being called, and he left the Metrodome's playing field. With only nine teammates around him, Dallas quarterback Danny White turned and handed off to halfback Tony Dorsett instead. When the Vikings saw the single-back set, they seemed to think the Cowboys were going with a slant play instead of a run. Adjusting accordingly, Minnesota failed to seal off the inside run.

Dorsett said he "saw a lot of green" as he took the ball in the backfield. . .and galloped 99 yards for a touchdown, setting an NFL record for the longest run from scrimmage.

Tony Dorsett made the best of a difficult situation simply by doing the task set before him. Though his team was outnumbered on that play, he did his own job—and he did it well. As the *New York Times* account of the game said, "It wound up as a record that can be broken only if the NFL lengthens its playing fields." The Cowboys ultimately lost the game, but that one play got them back into contention.

As believers, we will sometimes face battles in which we're outnumbered. God once called Gideon to take a mere three hundred men into battle against the vastly more numerous Midianites. But God gave Gideon a promise: "With the three hundred men. . .I will save you and give the Midianites into your hands" (Judges 7:7).

The shorthanded team won the day, just as God promised. He is on your side, too.

Let us hold unswervingly to the hope we profess,
for he who promised is faithful.
Hebrews 10:23

ALWAYS THE RIGHT CALL

The ball sailed too far right and into history.

In the 1986 season opener between the defending Super Bowl champion Chicago Bears and the Cleveland Browns, Bears center Jay Hilgenberg's errant snap on the third play from scrimmage flew past quarterback Jim McMahon deep into Chicago territory. The ball eventually bounced into the end zone, where Cleveland safety Al Gross recovered it before sliding out of bounds.

For the first time in NFL history, officials stopped the game to review the play on video. After consulting the tape, the ruling on the field stood: touchdown, Cleveland. Instant replay had been born. Thirteen years later, the NFL instituted sideline challenges, giving head coaches the power to request instant replay on close calls.

It's now official: We are an instant-replay nation.

The NFL introduced this technological tool to remove human error from officiating. But of course, even instant replay can't ensure the correct call all the time. (Anyone remember the infamous 2012 Seattle–Green Bay "Fail Mary" game, played with replacement referees?) Because of our sinful, fallen nature, anything humans are in charge of contains errors.

The Bible, however, is different. Yes, about forty different humans wrote the Bible, but the sixty-six books of scripture—from Genesis to Revelation—are the inerrant Word of God. That's because "all Scripture is God-breathed" (2 Timothy 3:16) and because the holy men who put pen to parchment "spoke from God as they were carried along by the Holy Spirit" (2 Peter 1:21).

Because God is the One who never lies (Titus 1:2), His words are "flawless" (today's verse), "pure" (Psalm 12:6 ESV), "right and true" (Psalm 33:4), and "eternal" (Psalm 119:89).

Trust in God's Word. Build your life upon it. The inspired, inerrant, and unchanging truths of scripture will never let you down. No instant replay needed.

"Every word of God is flawless."
PROVERBS 30:5

Born September 14, 1973, in St. Louis, Missouri

Played for Wisconsin Badgers
(1991–94)

Second-round pick in NFL Draft
by San Diego Chargers (1995)

Played running back for Chargers
(1995–2002)

5'8", 195 pounds

Pastor of City of Hope
International Church, San Diego

"When I took the chaplaincy over from a wonderful man of
God, Shawn Mitchell, one of the things he challenged me
with was this: 'Make sure you give them the Gospel of Jesus
Christ. Challenge their lives, because we don't want them
to just be good football players. We're called to help them
become godly men.'"

FULLY PROTECTED

Chicago Bears/Cardinals offensive lineman Dick Plasman is remembered as the last NFL player to go helmetless. The league mandated the piece of equipment in 1943, but he didn't don a helmet until 1947.

Here's the story.

Plasman played for the Bears from 1937 through 1941, when it was common to play without a helmet. He played offensive line, linebacker, and even kicker on occasion. He played a few games for the Bears in 1944, but it isn't clear if he wore a helmet for those games. But it's not likely because he took a break from football to serve in the military during World War II. When he returned from the war, he played for the Cardinals (1946–47) and "was the last man in the National Football League to play without a helmet, as late as 1947," according to an article in the *New York Times*.

Plasman wasn't happy about the rule change. The same article says he protested the rule, saying it would cause him hardship, even going so far as to claim that it was an unfair labor practice. The article says the league reconsidered and issued a special dispensation to Plasman, "comparable to baseball's exempting the old spitball pitchers when rules were changed while they were still active."

Dick Plasman's mind-set was a far cry from the current one in a league that is doing everything it can to protect players from head injuries. And that's the point of the rule. It was designed to protect him in spite of himself. In a similar fashion, Paul instructed the Ephesian church on how they should protect themselves: "Take up the shield of faith, with which you can extinguish all the flaming arrows of the evil one. Take the helmet of salvation and the sword of the Spirit, which is the word of God" (Ephesians 6:16–17).

> *"Harness the horses, mount the steeds! Take your positions with helmets on! Polish your spears, put on your armor!"*
> JEREMIAH 46:4

HARD WORK

Jerry Rice did not become the NFL's all-time leading receiver by talent alone. He worked.

In his 2010 Hall of Fame speech, Rice described how his father in rural Mississippi taught him to lay brick from 5:00 a.m. to dark. While on scaffolding, Rice would often catch bricks tossed up to him by his brothers, then deliver the bricks to his father. Because time was money, each move had a purpose. Rice approached his NFL service in much the same way.

Rice played sixteen years with the 49ers, finishing his twenty-year career in Oakland and Seattle. His fitness regimen was superb. He respected the game and gave it his all, an attitude that continues after his playing career.

In 2014, ten years after he retired from playing, Rice helped restore competition to the Pro Bowl. His hand-picked team of stars took on fellow Hall of Famer Deion Sanders's team, picking up a last-second, 22–21 victory.

"I hope the players today respect the game, respect the men whose shoulders they are standing on," Rice says. "But most importantly don't play for what the game can give them, rather what they can give to the game."

Rice is a hard worker with big numbers. He ranks as the top receiver in NFL history with 1,549 catches for 22,895 yards. His touchdown total of 208 is also the most ever for a receiver. Rice's other records are too numerous to list, but one is worth noting: his career total for Super Bowl receiving yards is 589, while second-place Lynn Swann is far behind at 364.

The Bible supports, and is filled with stories of, hard work. The people who rebuilt Jerusalem were wired that way (Nehemiah 4). So was Ruth (Ruth 2:6–7).

How does hard work suit you? Will hard work be part of your legacy?

The hardworking farmer should be the first
to receive a share of the crops.
2 TIMOTHY 2:6

UNSUNG MVPS: OFFENSIVE LINEMEN

Question: What do the Green Bay Packers of the 1960s, the Pittsburgh Steelers of the 1970s, the San Francisco 49ers of the 1980s, and the Dallas Cowboys of the 1990s all have in common?

The obvious answer is that all four were very talented teams that won multiple Super Bowl championships. But maybe a more important answer is that is that each of these teams featured strong offensive lines.

Most football fans can easily rattle off the names of "skill" players (players who throw, catch, and carry the ball) who have won championships. But when it comes to offensive linemen, only the most dedicated football geeks can name more than one or two players on each Super Bowl championship team.

Offensive linemen do the "dirty work" of protecting their quarterback and making room for their running backs to gain yards. A good offensive line can make good skill players great and great players into Super Bowl champions. But poor offensive line play can keep even the best quarterbacks, receivers, and running backs from performing to their abilities.

Yet in many ways, even the best offensive linemen labor in anonymity. More often than not, their names or numbers are mentioned only when starting lineups are announced—or when they commit a foul leading to a penalty on their team.

Most offensive linemen are good examples of contentedness in working without receiving personal glory. They are happy to do their work and not get their names mentioned in the headlines, knowing that when they do their jobs well, the whole team benefits.

How about you? Can you find satisfaction in your work for God—even when those around you don't recognize it? Absolutely you can—when you remember that what you do is for God's glory and for the benefit of others.

Do nothing out of selfish ambition or vain conceit. Rather, in humility value others above yourselves, not looking to your own interests but each of you to the interests of the others.
Philippians 2:3–4

THE BEAUTY OF ADOPTION

Human history is filled with famous adoptions. Caesar Augustus was adopted. So were Bill Clinton, John Lennon, Marilyn Monroe, Moses, Edgar Allen Poe, Babe Ruth, Mother Teresa, and Leo Tolstoy, among many others.

Count Colin Kaepernick among them.

In December 1987, Rick and Teresa Kaepernick adopted the future San Francisco 49ers quarterback, whose mother was nineteen and unmarried when he was born. The Kaepernicks already had two children but had lost two others to heart defects.

After Kaepernick dazzled at the University of Nevada, the 49ers selected him as a second-round draft pick in 2011. When a concussion sidelined veteran starter Alex Smith midway through the 2012 season, Kaepernick seized the opportunity, leading the 49ers all the way to Super Bowl XLVII. The following season, he guided San Francisco to the NFC Championship Game.

Kaepernick is a great adoption success story. But did you know that the same thing is true of every Christian?

When God saves us, He also spiritually adopts us, giving former rebels the full privileges of sons and daughters. Not only does He forgive our sins, but then He lavishes never-ending grace on us as beloved children (1 John 3:1). We are now "heirs of God and co-heirs with Christ" (Romans 8:17), recipients of current grace and a glorious future inheritance in eternity. Amazing!

God isn't a distant, uncaring deity. He is a loving heavenly Father who is near to His adopted children (Philippians 4:5) and who "delights in those who fear him" (Psalm 147:11). He is "compassionate and gracious, slow to anger, abounding in love" (Psalm 103:8). When we need Him, we can simply cry out, "Abba, Father!" and He will always hear us.

It's wonderful to be adopted by God!

The Spirit you received does not make you slaves, so that you live in fear again; rather, the Spirit you received brought about your adoption to sonship. And by him we cry, "Abba, Father."
ROMANS 8:15

DREAM REASSESSMENT

Hall of Famer Barry Sanders spent his entire career with the Detroit Lions, arguably one of the most subpar teams of the era. Sanders played ten seasons, from 1989 to '98, and was a Pro Bowler each year. His speed and elusiveness led him to the top five all-time in rushing. His conduct, both on and off the field, made him a fan favorite.

But Sanders startled fans in 1999 with the surprise announcement of his retirement. "My desire to exit the game is greater than my desire to remain in it," he said. Two years earlier, Sanders had signed a contract extension with the Lions and probably could have overtaken the top spot in career rushing yards. He had a lot to look forward to, but Sanders later said, "I quit because I didn't feel like the Detroit Lions had a chance to win. It just killed my enjoyment of the game."

Is it wrong to quit? Perhaps Sanders just found himself in need of a passion infusion. He had a goal of playing in the Super Bowl, but the Lions could never quite rise to that level. All the yards he consumed meant little if they couldn't get him to the big game. Sanders's exit signaled an end to one dream and a bridge to something new.

Sometimes in our lives—whether we've come short of our goals or even reached them—we sense that we aren't quite where we should be. But God always has a plan. We may just need to stop and listen for directions. "Be still, and know that I am God," we read in Psalm 46:10.

He may have something even better than records, awards, and money.

If any of you lacks wisdom, you should ask God,
who gives generously to all without finding fault, and it will
be given to you. But when you ask, you must believe and not doubt.
JAMES 1:5–6

PANCAKE MAN

In a 29–16 win over Notre Dame in 1996, Ohio State offensive lineman Orlando Pace pancaked seven defenders. Most offensive linemen are happy to neutralize a defender, but Pace took the game of football to a different level by routinely knocking defenders flat on their backs. That season, he became the first lineman since fellow Buckeye John Hicks (in 1972) to finish in the top four in Heisman Trophy voting.

The phrase "pancake block" didn't originate with Pace—some say it started with Bill Fralic of the Pittsburgh Panthers in 1983–84. But Pace eventually became known as the "Pancake Man," leading the way for his tailbacks to amass huge yardage. Eddie George, for example, ran for an Ohio State record 1,927 yards en route to the Heisman Trophy in 1995.

George gave a lot of the credit to Pace. "When situations were crucial, we always ran to his side," he told *Sports Illustrated*. "Every time I ran behind him was a guaranteed five yards, because he'd push his man that far backward. He's the best I've ever seen."

Pace went on to become a seven-time Pro Bowler in the NFL.

Usually, offensive linemen don't get many accolades from coaches or fans. Often they aren't noticed at all, unless they blow an assignment. But that doesn't deter the best of them. They find satisfaction knowing their efforts helped their team advance the ball.

The Christian life looks a lot like that. As we share the Gospel with our neighbors and serve in our church, we may not earn much attention. But there is satisfaction in obeying God, as Ephesians 6:7–8 says: "Serve wholeheartedly, as if you were serving the Lord, not people, because you know that the Lord will reward each one for whatever good they do."

Each of you should use whatever gift you have received to serve others,
as faithful stewards of God's grace in its various forms.
1 PETER 4:10

DON'T LET DEFEAT GET YOU DOWN

With impeccable credentials as a head coach, Bud Grant entered the NFL Hall of Fame in 1994. He was presented by a longtime friend, journalist Sid Hartman.

In 2012 the two men discussed what many people inevitably associate with the former Minnesota coach—the fact that four of his teams *lost* Super Bowls in the 1970s. Grant had a direct answer.

"Well, it probably bothers other people more than it bothers me," the eighteen-year coaching veteran said. "To survive in this business, you can't have a backwards look. You lose a game and then you have to move to the next one. You can't look back and say we could have, would have, should have. When it's over, it's over."

A man with a calm demeanor, Grant remained part of the Vikings organization well after his 1985 retirement. In 2014, his house in Bloomington became a magnet when he held a garage sale. Cameras caught the eighty-seven-year-old homeowner clearly enjoying himself.

Letting go of bitterness is the right thing to do. Raging at plays that made the Chiefs, Dolphins, Steelers, and Raiders Super Bowl champions is futile. Grant never let defeat consume him.

His teams were known for their discipline. Christians should be known for the same—and that takes effort. When we don't allow God to work His peace in us, we can end up like Jonah. He was mad that God had spared the city of Nineveh, which repented at Jonah's own preaching. Then he was mad at the death of a plant he was using for shade. "Is it right for you to be angry about the plant?" God asked. "It is," Jonah replied. "And I'm so angry I wish I were dead" (Jonah 4:9).

Don't go there. Let the Holy Spirit chip away at your old, sinful nature. Leave bitterness in the dust.

Get rid of all bitterness, rage and anger.
Ephesians 4:31

"YOU WILL BE THE ONES"

One of the more cryptic statements in college football came from Michigan State coach Mark Dantonio, who in December of 2012 told his underclassmen at the team banquet, "You will be the ones."

The 2012 Spartans were a .500 team. They had grown accustomed to failing to win their league championship and advance to the Rose Bowl. It last happened in 1987—twenty-five long years previous.

Some of the players were confused, but Dantonio was not. He saw them as winners.

"You will be the ones."

So the Spartans stepped out into their 2013 season and began to win. They won so often that they qualified for the league championship game against highly regarded Ohio State. After beating the Buckeyes, "the ones" capped it all off by defeating Stanford in the Rose Bowl.

The Dantonio college football prophecy may be properly characterized as amazing, but the prophecies of God in the Bible over those He claims as His are even more spectacular. Those of us who are in Christ, born from above, believers in His blood as a cleansing agent for sin, are called "saints," or "holy ones." God does this in the process of regeneration. In effect, He says to all Christians, "You will be the ones who pass from darkness to light, from death to life, by the power that makes all things new."

Christians possess something much greater than the Rose Bowl trophy; we possess God's Holy Spirit. We will be the ones to be awarded the prize.

It is good to focus on that (see Ephesians 1:18–23). To God be the glory for His mysterious manner of salvation!

Therefore, my brothers and sisters, make every effort to confirm your calling and election. For if you do these things, you will never stumble.
2 PETER 1:10

AGE IS JUST A NUMBER

Rich Gannon's story isn't typical of a successful NFL quarterback. Most great NFL signal-callers are high draft choices teams bring in for the purpose of rebuilding a team or to groom as a replacement for an aging veteran.

Gannon's story is different because he did his best work after the age of thirty-four—high middle age in quarterback years. And he did it after being benched, traded, or cast aside to fend for himself as a free agent.

Through it all, Gannon—a man of faith who believed God had a plan for his NFL career—never gave up on his dream of success in the NFL. He remained patient, kept himself in shape, and made himself available to any team that showed interest.

After the New England Patriots drafted and traded Gannon (the 98th pick out of the University of Delaware) in 1987, he knocked around the league for eleven seasons, enjoying some success for the Minnesota Vikings and the Kansas City Chiefs. But then Gannon caught fire with the Oakland Raiders.

Over four seasons (1999–2002), Gannon was one of the best in the league, earning four trips to the Pro Bowl (winning the game's Most Valuable Player award in 2000 and 2001) and being named MVP of the entire league in 2002. He still holds several Raider team passing records, including the most yards in a season (4,689 in 2002). He led the Raiders to playoff appearances in 2000 and 2001, and Oakland finished the 2002 season with a loss to the Tampa Bay Buccaneers in Super Bowl XXXVII.

Rich Gannon stands as one of the NFL's examples of how good things can happen to those who are willing to work hard and remain patient as they wait for God's blessings—even if it means waiting until later in life to receive them.

Wait for the Lord; be strong and take heart and wait for the Lord.
PSALM 27:14

"CLOUD OF WITNESSES"

Though the NFL claims the most fans, college football boasts the larger stadiums. Several university venues offer considerably more seating than their pro football counterparts—though those seats are sometimes in packed bleacher sections.

Exact figures vary by source, but New York's MetLife Stadium—home of the Giants and Jets—is acknowledged as the largest NFL stadium with a capacity nearing 83,000. More than a dozen college fields, however, accommodate larger crowds.

Michigan Stadium, where the Wolverines play, is the granddaddy of all football facilities with a capacity of nearly 110,000. Fellow Big Ten member Penn State's Beaver Stadium is close behind, with more than 107,000 seats. After that are three facilities in the 102,000 range: Tennessee's Neyland Stadium, Texas A&M's Kyle Field (after an enormous 40,000-seat expansion started in 2013), and the famed "Horseshoe" of Ohio State. Alabama's Bryant-Denny Stadium and Darrell K. Royal–Texas Memorial Stadium (home of the Longhorns) round out the 100,000-plus fields. The rest of the bigger-than-NFL stadiums include Los Angeles Memorial Coliseum, home of the USC Trojans; Georgia's Sanford Stadium; LSU's Tiger Stadium; UCLA's Rose Bowl; Florida's Ben Hill Griffin Stadium; and Auburn's Jordan-Hare Stadium.

On any given Saturday, millions will watch college football from a stadium seat or on television. To borrow a biblical phrase, that's "a great cloud of witnesses."

It was the unnamed writer of Hebrews who first penned those words. Following the description of fifteen named and countless unnamed heroes in chapter 11's "Faith Hall of Fame," the author urged his readers, "Since we are surrounded by such a great cloud of witnesses, let us throw off everything that hinders and the sin that so easily entangles. And let us run with perseverance the race marked out for us" (Hebrews 12:1).

In the great race of life, some are cheering us on. . .and others seek hope in our example. Are you running your race with perseverance?

Let us not become weary in doing good.
GALATIANS 6:9

FAITHFUL IN SMALL THINGS

In an age when football is on television every Thursday, Friday, Saturday, Sunday, and Monday, it's hard to imagine a time before the game was so accessible. You might be surprised to learn that the first televised NFL game—played on October 22, 1939, in New York at Ebbets Field in front of 13,057 fans—was broadcast to approximately five hundred TV sets.

The Brooklyn Dodgers defeated the Philadelphia Eagles 23–14 that day. Broadcaster Allen "Skip" Walz worked without a monitor and NBC used only two Iconoscope cameras.

"I did my own spotting and when the play moved up and down the field, on punts and kickoffs, I'd point to tell the cameraman what I'd be talking about and we used hand signals to communicate," Walz said in a *Football Digest* article. "The other camera was on the field, at the 50-yard line, but it couldn't move so we didn't use it much."

Football broadcasting has come a long way since then. Early in the 2014 season, CBS was drawing 19.5 million viewers for its Sunday afternoon games, and Fox was drawing 20.5 million. NBC was drawing 21.8 million on Sunday nights, and ESPN was drawing 9.4 million on Monday night.

What started as a small venture has grown exponentially. That's exactly what Jesus told His disciples would happen when we can be trusted with small kingdom matters. "Whoever can be trusted with very little can also be trusted with much, and whoever is dishonest with very little will also be dishonest with much," He said in Luke 16:10. How are you doing with the little things?

Now it is required that those who
have been given a trust must prove faithful.
1 CORINTHIANS 4:2

TRUST AND LOVE

How does today's National Football League differ from that of earlier generations? According to Jim David, a Detroit cornerback of the 1950s, players had more trust in their teammates. "We believed in each other," David said.

Players of that era seemed to experience a different team dynamic, one that included deeper friendships. Certainly, players were less famous and wealthy, often holding jobs in the off-season to support their "hobby" of playing professional football. In 1958, the average annual salary for players was $10,000.

Another Detroiter of the fifties, Jim Doran, trusted his team and the Lions returned the favor. When facing the Browns in the 1953 NFL championship game, Doran—known for defense but pressed into service as a wide receiver—told quarterback Bobby Layne that he could get behind his Cleveland opponent and take the ball in for a touchdown. Layne used short passes to manage much of the game, seemingly lulling the Browns to sleep before he and Doran launched a 33-yard score. The PAT gave Detroit a shocking 17–16 lead, and the Lions held the Browns in the final two minutes to win the title.

"Jimmy Doran don't tell lies," Layne said later. "If he says he can get deep, you better get him the ball."

Trust and love are inseparable—trust leads to love, and there's no real love without trust. Biblically speaking, "[Love] always protects, always trusts, always hopes, always perseveres" (1 Corinthians 13:7).

If trust and love are important on the football field, imagine what they must mean in our relationship with God, our spouse, or our kids.

What can you do today to build trust and love into your relationships?

[Jesus said], "'Love the Lord your God with all your heart and with all your soul and with all your strength and with all your mind';
and, 'Love your neighbor as yourself.'"
Luke 10:27

THE UNCHANGEABLE SAVIOR

A touchdown hasn't always been worth six points in professional football, nor has a field goal always earned a team three points.

In 1892, a touchdown was worth four points and a field goal was worth five, which begs two questions—one serious and the other not so much. Why even try to score a touchdown if you could kick a field goal and earn more points? And did anybody who gathered in a wings establishment in 1892 jump up and down and scream about his or her favorite team scoring on a "pick four" (as opposed to a "pick six")? Probably not.

In 1897, touchdowns were increased to five points. And in 1904, field goals were reduced to four points and then to three points in 1909. Three years later, the value of a touchdown was finally increased to six points.

For more than a hundred years, those point values have stood—rewarding teams twice the number of points for advancing the ball into the end zone as the number they receive when a drive falls short and they have to settle for the field goal. And that seems about right, doesn't it? Maybe that's why those standards have remained in place over the last century.

Standards in football have been set through trial and error, but thankfully, Jesus never changes. Hebrews 13:8 says, "Jesus Christ is the same yesterday and today and forever." He loves humanity today as much as He did a thousand years ago, and a thousand years before that. And His standards are just as true now as they were in the beginning.

God, who is enthroned from of old, who does not change—he will hear them and humble them, because they have no fear of God.
PSALM 55:19

UNEXPECTED HEROES

Tom Brady's surprising rise to NFL superstardom has been well documented. But it's so remarkable, it bears repeating.

After two solid—but unspectacular—years as the University of Michigan's starting quarterback, Brady was selected by the New England Patriots with the 199th overall pick of the 2000 draft. The quarterbacks taken ahead of him were Chad Pennington (18th), Giovanni Carmazzi (65th), Chris Redman (75th), Tee Martin (163rd), and Marc Bulger (168th). Kind of puts things in perspective, huh?

Four Super Bowl victories, thirteen playoff appearances, eleven Pro Bowls, and multiple passing records later (as of the end of the 2015 season), Brady is widely recognized as a surefire Hall of Famer and one of the top five greatest quarterbacks in NFL history. Not bad for a sixth-round draft pick.

Brady came out of nowhere to do great things. That pretty much sums up every Christian's life, too. You might not be headed for a 5,000-yard passing season in the NFL, but if you're a believer, you started life without grand expectations or anything to boast about. As Ephesians 2:1 says, "You were dead in your transgressions and sins."

When God calls people for His purposes, He chooses the "foolish," "weak," "lowly," and "despised" (1 Corinthians 1:27–28). This is so He gets all the glory, not us. You see, God doesn't choose people to serve Him based on *our* prior reputation or merits. He chooses us based on *His* mercy and grace.

So if you're feeling insignificant, like God can never use you, take heart. You're in a prime position to do great things for Him. Humble yourself before the Lord, watch Him work mightily in your life, and marvel at His unexpected goodness.

God chose the lowly things of this world and the despised things—
and the things that are not—to nullify the things that are,
so that no one may boast before him.
1 Corinthians 1:28–29

IT'S A WAR (KIND OF)

In his famous (and very funny) monologue about the differences between baseball and football, comedian George Carlin used terms such as "field general" (the quarterback), "aerial assault," "deadly accuracy," "the blitz," "bullet passes and long bombs," "sustained ground attack," and "punching holes in the forward line of the enemy's defensive line."

We've all heard commentators, players, and coaches prefacing a big game by saying something along the lines of "It's going to be a war out there." Of course, football isn't literal war—no bullets are flying and no one is dropping real bombs on people. Football is just a game, and outside of some very rare instances, no one is dying on football fields on Friday nights or Saturday and Sunday afternoons.

Still, the two are similar in so many ways that the language of football includes countless references to war.

The game of football and the Christian life are a lot alike, aren't they?

The Bible teaches that believers are to be engaged in spiritual warfare and that we are to cover ourselves in several defensive weapons—the belt of truth, the breastplate of righteousness, the Gospel of peace, the shield of faith, and the helmet of salvation—as well as one weapon of offense, the Word of God (see Ephesians 6:14–17).

No football player in his right mind would think of going out on the field without his protective gear—his shoulder pads, hip pads, knee pads, or helmet. And no follower of Christ should go out into the world without the protective gear God has provided us.

After all, it's a war out there!

Put on the full armor of God, so that you can take your stand against the devil's schemes. For our struggle is not against flesh and blood, but against the rulers, against the authorities, against the powers of this dark world and against the spiritual forces of evil in the heavenly realms.
EPHESIANS 6:11–12

Born July 6, 1953, in Wallace, Idaho

Played for University of Alabama Crimson Tide (1971–74)

USC Trojans offensive coordinator/quarterbacks coach (1993–96)

Oregon State Beavers head coach (1997–98)

San Diego Chargers head coach (1999–2001)

New Orleans Saints assistant coach (2002)

Oregon State Beavers head coach (2003–2014)

Nebraska Cornhuskers head coach (2015–)

"There's a misunderstanding about Christianity in some areas and it goes like this: *If you're a Christian, you're not a tough guy.* I've found that to be absolutely untrue. We've been given the advice in scripture that whatever we do, we're to do it heartily for Him. To me, if you're playing football and doing it heartily for the Lord, if you're doing it the way the game is supposed to be played, then you're playing in a tough, physical fashion."

AT THE REQUEST OF A PRESIDENT

Some observers were describing football as "barbaric." Perhaps they were right.

Newspapers reported at the end of the 1905 season that *nineteen* players had died from football injuries. Earlier that fall, President Theodore Roosevelt met with college representatives to seek greater sportsmanship within the game. Shortly after that meeting, it was reported that Roosevelt's own son had been injured preparing for a game at Harvard.

In November, Columbia University shelved its football season because of the growing number of player injuries and deaths. By December, more than sixty colleges were discussing a new rules committee to improve the safety of the game. In March 1906, the Intercollegiate Athletic Association of the United States (IAAUS) was established. This organization would come to be known as the National Collegiate Athletic Association (NCAA).

Rules created at the college level would also impact the development of professional football. The American Professional Football Association (later known as the National Football League) began in 1920 with Jim Thorpe as its first president. This new league would need recognized standards, too.

Today, we take protective rules and safety gear for granted. . .and life-threatening injuries, while still possible, are rare. Over the years, thousands upon thousands of players have benefited from the drive for better sportsmanship and safety, and it started at the request of a president.

Sometimes it's difficult to step forward to encourage the right thing. Change can be tough, and sometimes people resist it. But God has always called us to do right and to help others. As Proverbs 31:8 says, "Speak up for those who cannot speak for themselves."

God can use your words and actions to make a positive change in the world.

> *He has shown you, O mortal, what is good. And what does*
> *the LORD require of you? To act justly and to love mercy*
> *and to walk humbly with your God.*
> MICAH 6:8

BOUNCING BACK

Three NFL quarterbacks have been sacked a dozen times in one game—Bert Jones (1980, by the Rams), Warren Moon (1985, by the Cowboys), and Donovan McNabb (2007, by the Giants). To put that into perspective, Peyton Manning was sacked just eighteen times in 2013 while leading the league in passing yardage. And Drew Brees was sacked twenty-six times in 2012 while also leading the league in yards passing.

McNabb did the honorable thing when he was sacked twelve times, taking a long, hard look at his own game. "It's easy to point fingers, but you've got to point it at yourself to see if you could've done better. You've got to be a man, step up," he said.

The truth is, for each of these quarterbacks, it was just one bad game—one most fans don't even remember. Jones played in the Pro Bowl in 1976 and was named Associated Press and United Press International Most Valuable Player that same season. He ended up throwing for more than 18,000 yards in his career. Moon had an incredible career in the CFL and NFL, going to the Pro Bowl nine times and throwing for nearly 50,000 yards in the NFL alone. McNabb went to six Pro Bowls, throwing for more than 37,000 yards.

These quarterbacks didn't let one bad day define their careers. As believers, we can't allow one sin to define our spiritual lives. First John 1:9 gives us the remedy for bouncing back strong: "If we confess our sins, he is faithful and just and will forgive us our sins and purify us from all unrighteousness." Unconfessed sin can lead to more sin, which eventually leads to entrapment.

Godly sorrow brings repentance that leads to salvation and leaves no regret, but worldly sorrow brings death.
2 CORINTHIANS 7:10

A MORE PASSIONATE DEFENSE

After an All-America career at North Texas State, "Mean Joe" Greene considered his thirteen years in the NFL postgraduate work.

A first-round draft choice of the Pittsburgh Steelers in 1969, the defensive tackle suffered through a 1–13 train wreck his first season. But his ruthless pursuit of winning became a rallying cry to team veterans. Under Greene's leadership, Pittsburgh would go on to win four Super Bowl titles through the 1970s.

For Joe Greene, the game of football was a consuming passion. Opposing coaches would double- and triple-team the 6'4", 275-pound cornerstone of Pittsburgh's fearsome "Steel Curtain."

Greene was named the 1969 Defensive Rookie of the Year, received Pro Bowl invitations ten times, and was inducted into the Pro Football Hall of Fame in 1987. After his playing days, he served as an assistant coach for the Steelers, as well as the Miami Dolphins and Arizona Cardinals. He would then return to the Steelers' front office, serving through two more Super Bowl championships. As both a player and coach in the Steelers' system, Greene is a rare owner of *six* Super Bowl rings.

"The thing, I think, that sets Joe aside from everybody is his attitude," coach Chuck Noll said during Greene's Hall of Fame enshrinement. "It is something that you don't do anything to get—it is something that you have, you have deep down in. He had all kinds of attitude, probably the best. He wanted to play the game very badly."

As Christians, are we as committed to our cause? Do we have Joe Greene's attitude when it comes to following Jesus? The apostle Paul certainly did. Let's follow his game plan in 1 Corinthians 16:13: "Be on your guard; stand firm in the faith; be courageous; be strong."

> *Let us not become weary in doing good, for at the proper time we will reap a harvest if we do not give up.*
> GALATIANS 6:9

THE SELFLESS LEGACY

It is practically unheard of for an NFL career to be defined in terms of milestones others achieved. Who could accomplish such a thing? Only a selfless player.

Fullback is a selfless position. Some teams don't use a fullback anymore, due to the growth of the spread offense, but those that do expect their fullback to block well. Howard Griffith, who played the position professionally from 1991 through 2001, was one of the best.

Griffith rushed for just 351 yards for his career, but his legacy rests on the fact that he valued others above his own personal statistics. Five different featured backs who played with him became 1,000-yard rushers. In football terms, by any measure of consistency and excellence in blocking, Griffith led.

Griffith's blocking helped the Denver Broncos win two Super Bowls. Typically he was the fifth option for quarterback John Elway in the passing game, but he still managed to make big receptions for crucial gains in dramatic moments. All of this earned Griffith a reputation as a good teammate.

Way back in college, as a featured back for the University of Illinois, Griffith scored eight touchdowns in a game. He knew glory that way. But glory is fleeting. As a pro, he knew humility.

Jesus knew amazing glory, too. He had an indescribable amount of it with His Father, but He mysteriously set some aside to walk among us. That required humility.

Jesus said the poor in spirit would be blessed because the kingdom of heaven is theirs (see Matthew 5:3). How well is your poverty of spirit, your selflessness, being displayed? How well do you love others and put them ahead of yourself?

Do nothing out of selfish ambition or vain conceit.
Rather, in humility value others above yourselves.
PHILIPPIANS 2:3

COMPLETE IN CHRIST

Throwing seven touchdown passes in one game might sound like video game numbers, but eight real-life NFL players have accomplished the feat: Sid Luckman (1943), Adrian Burk (1954), George Blanda (1961), Y. A. Tittle (1961), Joe Kapp (1969), Peyton Manning (2013), Nick Foles (2013), and Drew Brees (2015).

Luckman, who was the first to pass for seven TDs, did so out of T-formation. Not surprisingly, Burk ended up leading the league in touchdown passes the year he threw seven in one game. Blanda, who was also a kicker, tacked on seven PATs the day he threw seven touchdown passes. Tittle once made the following comment when seeing a picture of himself from his special day: "I didn't know I was that good." Kapp's accomplishment came opposite of the great Johnny Unitas of the Baltimore Colts, prompting Kapp to say he asked for Unitas's autograph after the game. Manning was thirty-seven when he tossed seven touchdown passes. When Foles learned he had tied the record, he called it an honor. Brees told ESPN he'd never been part of something like that.

In the Bible, the number seven often signifies completion or perfection. God rested on the seventh day. A week has seven days. John addressed seven churches in the book of Revelation. The book of Joshua (6:15–20) tells us that on the seventh day, Joshua and his army marched around the city of Jericho seven times, as the Lord had instructed, and with trumpets blaring and Joshua's men shouting, the walls came down.

The next time a player sets a new record for accomplishing a task seven times, think about the finished work of Christ that completes and perfects you before a holy God.

For in Christ all the fullness of the Deity lives in bodily form,
and in Christ you have been brought to fullness.
COLOSSIANS 2:9–10

A "SPECIAL" PLAYER

How does a National Football League wide receiver who finishes his twelve-year career with 51 receptions for 779 yards and nine touchdowns end up being thought of so highly that many fans and writers believe he belongs in the Pro Football Hall of Fame?

By being the best ever at what he did—namely, playing special teams.

Steve Tasker spent most of his NFL career with Buffalo and was a key player on the Bills teams that won four straight American Football Conference championships in the early 1990s. But it wasn't his work as a receiver that made him such a special player. Rather, it was his role on the Bills special teams that makes him so memorable.

Tasker, who stood 5 feet, 9 inches tall and weighed around 189 pounds during his playing days, was a feared hitter and tackler on Buffalo's kickoff and punt teams, and he had a knack for blocking kicks and making big plays on the punt and field goal defense teams. As the ultimate "specialist," he was such a factor for the Bills that then–Buffalo coach Marv Levy thought of him as one of the Bills' most important players—right up there with quarterback Jim Kelly, running back Thurman Thomas, and wide receiver Andre Reed.

Just as Steve Tasker made a huge impact in a "lesser" role in the NFL, we too can make an impact for God's kingdom, even if we don't play what we might consider a big role. So whatever God has called you to do, do it with passion and work to be the best you can be.

Whatever you do, work at it with all your heart, as working for
the Lord, not for human masters, since you know that you
will receive an inheritance from the Lord as a reward.
It is the Lord Christ you are serving.
Colossians 3:23–24

STAND FIRM

For more than sixty years, the National Football League has been a solid (if not booming) operation. Not since 1952, when the Dallas Texans folded after a single season, has an NFL team gone out of business.

Of course, some NFL teams have moved from one city to another—for example, the Cleveland Browns becoming the Baltimore Ravens in 1996. But consider the following teams from the past that just didn't make it.

The Dayton Triangles played ten seasons (1920–29), starting out as a college basketball team that transitioned to pro football. The Duluth Kelleys (1923–27), named after the Kelley-Duluth Hardware Store, struggled to play home games in the frigid conditions of Minnesota. The Providence Steam Rollers had a winning tradition, earning the NFL championship in 1928; they played in a stadium designed for bicycle racing before folding in 1933.

Many teams lasted just one season—or less. The Kenosha Maroons managed only five games in 1924 and lost them all. The Buffalo-area Tonawanda Kardex played exactly *one* NFL game. Other "one and done" seasons were recorded by the Brooklyn Lions, St. Louis Gunners, Hartford Blues, and Louisville Colonels.

What is it that allows some franchises to stand firm and succeed over time? Having fans in the stands is a key. And that's more likely with a team full of disciplined players executing well. And that's more likely with a good coach who really understands success.

It's similar with the life of the Christian. We have a great (actually, *perfect*) Coach. When we follow His lead, we'll win. . .and He'll make sure we last. As the apostle Paul told the Philippians, "He who began a good work in you will carry it on to completion until the day of Christ Jesus" (Philippians 1:6).

Stand firm then, with the belt of truth buckled around your waist. . .
and the sword of the Spirit, which is the word of God.
Ephesians 6:14, 17

LIFE OVER DEATH

Marshall University learned how to walk through the valley of the shadow of death.

Football at Marshall nearly came to an end in 1970 when most of its team was killed in the crash of Southern Airways Flight 932. Coaches, fans, and boosters also perished in the worst air tragedy in NCAA history. For the school in Huntington, West Virginia, life would never be the same.

Every November 14 the community commemorates the seventy-five lives lost. A wreath is laid and a memorial fountain, dedicated in 1972, is turned off until the following spring. A nearby bronze plaque reads, "They shall live on in the hearts of their families and friends forever, and this memorial records their loss to the university and to the community."

In the aftermath of the tragedy, some suggested that Marshall simply drop its football program. But the choice was made to rebuild the team, a decision helped by the NCAA's special permission to allow freshmen to play varsity. With a handful of older players who were not on the doomed plane, the "Young Thundering Herd" not surprisingly struggled to a 9–33 record over the next four years. Marshall did, however, win its first home game after the plane crash, a 15–13 come-from-behind victory over Xavier.

The Herd kept pressing forward, eventually becoming a Division I-AA powerhouse in the 1980s, and a solid Division I program in the late 1990s. The school has produced NFL talent like Chad Pennington, Byron Leftwich, and Randy Moss.

Marshall is a picture of life after death, one of the great themes of scripture. "Death has been swallowed up in victory," wrote the apostle Paul in 1 Corinthians 15:54, quoting Isaiah 25:8. Death is inevitable, but in Jesus Christ, it's simply the gateway to the perfect life of heaven.

Even though I walk through the darkest valley, I will fear no evil,
for you are with me; your rod and your staff, they comfort me.
PSALM 23:4

ONE WELL-PLACED STEP

Lamar Hunt loved Dallas and applied to the National Football League to get a franchise for his city. That request was denied not once, but twice. Convinced that Dallas needed a professional football team, Hunt looked to baseball to find a solution. If baseball could have two leagues, why couldn't pro football? A few conversations later, franchises for an all-new "American Football League" were in place for Dallas, Houston, Denver, Los Angeles, New York, and Minneapolis.

When the NFL analyzed this new Hunt-led organization, it quickly counteracted the move by franchising a Dallas team. The Cowboys would play their first game the same year as Hunt's Texans. The Texans found success quickly, going 8–6 their first year and 11–3 their third season, when they won the AFL title. But the next year, Hunt chose to move the team to Kansas City, a community without pro football. The Texans/Chiefs became the most successful AFL franchise of the 1960s.

Hunt, the son of oil tycoon H. L. Hunt, had an interest in other sports as well. He helped to make soccer an accepted stadium event in America, and a major soccer tournament is named after him. He also promoted basketball, tennis, and ice hockey.

"When you walked in a room and. . .saw he was a part of something," New England Patriots owner Robert Kraft said of Hunt, "you knew it was something that was branded with integrity and solid and something you could stand behind."

All of Hunt's achievements started with a vision, followed by a step, not unlike the image presented in Psalm 119:105: "Your word is a lamp for my feet, a light on my path." If God has given you a vision for your life, family, ministry, or job, shine His light on your path. . .and take the first step.

In their hearts humans plan their course,
but the LORD establishes their steps.
PROVERBS 16:9

HELP NEEDED

September 2014 was the NFL's nightmare month.

As the 2014 season kicked off, many observers were accusing the NFL of being too lenient toward Carolina Panthers defensive end Greg Hardy and Baltimore Ravens running back Ray Rice, both of whom had gone to court earlier that year on domestic violence charges. The league was also tracking a police investigation into a domestic abuse charge against San Francisco 49ers defensive tackle Ray McDonald.

On Saturday, September 13, right before Week 2's games, news broke that Minnesota Vikings superstar running back Adrian Peterson had been indicted on a child abuse charge. Two days later, TMZ.com aired previously unseen video footage of Rice knocking his then-fiancée unconscious the previous February in a hotel elevator in Atlantic City, New Jersey. Then, on September 17, Arizona Cardinals running back Jonathan Dwyer was arrested on domestic violence charges.

It was an all-out public relations disaster for the NFL. But the news shouldn't have been surprising. Pro football, just like any other sport, is simply a reflection of society in general. The world is a dark, sinful place, filled with all manner of rebellion against the Creator.

Ever since humanity's fall into sin (see Genesis 3), all mankind has inherited a sinful nature from Adam (see Romans 5:12). Humans are thoroughly corrupt in thought, word, and deed—unable to please God on their own (today's verse). Left to our sinful state, we have nothing of any spiritual value to offer God. This is sometimes called the doctrine of total depravity.

But there is hope. In His great love, God responded to our helpless condition not with wrath and condemnation, but with mercy and compassion. He sent His Son to pay for our sins. Now, through faith in Jesus, we can be saved from our hopeless condition. Praise God for helping the helpless!

"All have turned away, they have together become worthless;
there is no one who does good, not even one."
ROMANS 3:12

SMALL IS OKAY

The landscape of America is filled with small colleges that play football. Some play at the Division II level, some at Division III. Some are NAIA schools. Many carry the label "private liberal arts." Little is how they roll.

Many games are played on quaint, picturesque campuses where the venue is far less pressurized than it is inside a major college or NFL stadium. The players compete hard before hundreds or maybe a few thousand fans, and news about their feats often does not travel beyond their homespun environment or little-known conference. For most, this is how the sport ends. The day of small things is all they know.

In the hills and woodlands of Rock Island, Illinois, a 115-acre campus hugs the Mississippi River and presents itself as one of these typical settings for out-of-the-way football. Augustana College, with an enrollment of about twenty-five hundred students, plays at the Division III level. It is tucked away, quiet yet not despised. Let's just say that its identity, meek and lowly, has meaning. Someone was discovered there.

He is one of the better quarterbacks in NFL history, and he came from Augustana. His name is Ken Anderson, and he played sixteen seasons (1971–86) with the Cincinnati Bengals. Kenny, as he is sometimes known, won four league passing titles and threw for 32,838 yards over the course of his career. His historical significance is that he stands as an original—the first quarterback minted by Bill Walsh as a classic coin in the West Coast offense.

Being from a small school never harmed Kenny Anderson. One of his former teammates, Pete Johnson, calls him "a football player. He didn't care about being famous."

The testimony of the small can say it all.

"Who dares despise the day of small things, since the seven eyes of the Lord that range throughout the earth will rejoice when they see the chosen capstone in the hand of Zerubbabel?"
ZECHARIAH 4:10

EQUIPPED TO LAST

It is a rare NFL lineman who can put up with the pounding for twenty years. Call him reliable, dependable, and consistent. Or maybe just call him blessed.

Jackie Slater was all of that for one organization. He was an offensive tackle who played his entire career for the Rams—nineteen years in Los Angeles and one in St. Louis. He played 259 games, the most ever for an NFL offensive lineman at the time of his retirement, and he blocked for seven different 1,000-yard rushers, including Eric Dickerson and Jerome Bettis.

In his Hall of Fame speech, Slater credited his longevity to good health, good coaches and teammates, and a driving desire to be the best. But then he added, "I'm thankful to my Lord and Savior Jesus Christ. . . . I know that God provided it all."

Minus a lot of contact, an NFL player occasionally plays twenty or more years. Most of them are kickers or punters. But there is another one like Slater who survived a lot of mayhem: Hall of Fame cornerback Darrell Green also spent twenty years with one organization. His take on how he managed that, with the Washington Redskins, is similar to Slater's. "God had a plan for me," Green said. "I stayed the course."

God wants us all to endure, whether in football, our marriages, our ethics, or our faith. When we do, we show others the character of God Himself, who "reigns forever" (Psalm 9:7). And He's the One who equips us to endure!

Now may the God of peace, who through the blood of the eternal
covenant brought back from the dead our Lord Jesus, that great Shepherd
of the sheep, equip you with everything good for doing his will,
and may he work in us what is pleasing to him, through Jesus Christ,
to whom be glory for ever and ever. Amen.
HEBREWS 13:20–21

KING OF THE COMEBACK

Denver Broncos fans from the John Elway era know all about nail biters.

Elway seemed at his best when the game was at its worst. Time after time, the games he managed would appear to be getting away. But Elway, a first-round draft choice in 1983, often responded by mounting a dramatic comeback. Forty-seven times in his career he overcame overwhelming odds by leading a fourth-quarter game-tying or game-winning drive—including "*The* Drive," a 98-yard touchdown march in the 1986 AFC Championship that broke the heart of every Cleveland Browns fan.

One of the best quarterbacks in the history of the game, Elway understood perseverance. "I think you learn better when things are done the hard way," he once said.

Elway retired with stats that raised the bar for all future quarterbacks. He won back-to-back Super Bowls (in 1998 and '99), earning the Most Valuable Player award in the latter. He was selected to nine Pro Bowl teams. He threw for 300 touchdowns, rushed for 33 more, and even scored once as a receiver. No matter what difficulties his Broncos faced, John Elway was looking for one more opportunity to win. That determination brought him to a place where comebacks were almost expected.

But it took effort, just like success in life does. While it may seem easier to give up than get up, to lie down than walk tall, don't quit! As the apostle Paul said in Romans 12:12, "Be joyful in hope, patient in affliction, faithful in prayer."

In all these things we are more than conquerors through him who loved us. For I am convinced that neither death nor life, neither angels nor demons, neither the present nor the future, nor any powers, neither height nor depth, nor anything else in all creation, will be able to separate us from the love of God that is in Christ Jesus our Lord.
ROMANS 8:37–39

SAM BRADFORD, QUARTERBACK

Born November 8, 1987, in Oklahoma City, Oklahoma

Played for University of Oklahoma Sooners (2007–09)

All-American, Heisman Trophy winner (2008)

No. 1 pick in NFL Draft by St. Louis Rams (2010)

NFL Offensive Rookie of the Year (2010)

NFL record for most completions by a rookie (2010)

Played for Rams (2010–2014), Eagles (2015–)

6'4", 226 pounds, throws right

"I first need to thank God. He has given me so many blessings, He's blessed me with so many opportunities, and He's put so many wonderful people in my life that I give all the credit to Him. Without Him, I'd be nowhere and we'd all be nowhere." (from Heisman Trophy acceptance speech, 2008)

CELEBRATE. . .CAREFULLY

It didn't change the outcome of Super Bowl XXVII—not by a long shot—but it established the reputation of Cowboys Pro Bowl defensive lineman Leon Lett as a player who (let's put this gently) often fell victim to his own mental lapses.

The Cowboys led the Buffalo Bills big in the fourth quarter when Lett scooped up a fumble and headed toward the end zone. But around the five-yard line, he held the ball out in his right hand and slowed down, sure he would cross the goal line untouched.

Then came one of the most cringe-worthy moments in NFL history: Bills wide receiver Don Beebe, who never gave up on the play, caught Lett around the two and knocked the ball out of his enormous hand. It rolled into the end zone and out of bounds for a touchback.

Fortunately for Lett, his infamous gaffe didn't cost his team. (The Cowboys won 52–17.) However, on a more personal level, the fumble and touchback is now listed on nearly every sportswriter's list of Super Bowl follies. And when anyone mentions the name "Leon Lett," it's the first thing that comes to mind.

Lett's mistake on that play wasn't celebrating as he crossed the goal line for another Cowboys touchdown—NFL players do that all the time. His mistake was celebrating *carelessly*, in "showboating" instead of finishing what he started when he picked up the fumble and started rumbling toward the end zone.

It was an embarrassing moment for Lett—and an object lesson for those of us who follow Jesus Christ.

God has given people who live and work for Him many occasions for celebration. But we should never allow ourselves to become complacent or careless as we celebrate, but instead remember that we have tasks to complete before we receive our final reward.

Now finish the work, so that your eager willingness to do it may be matched by your completion of it, according to your means.
2 Corinthians 8:11

RIVALRIES

College football teams play around a dozen games per year. But there's often one game on the schedule that's make-or-break.

A team could finish 12–1 and see their season as a failure—if that single loss was to a hated rival. But upsetting a rival can turn a losing season into a rousing success.

Here's how Yahoo Sports ranked the ten best rivalries in college football: (1) Alabama vs. Auburn; (2) Ohio State vs. Michigan; (3) Oklahoma vs. Texas; (4) Army vs. Navy; (5) USC vs. Notre Dame; (6) Miami vs. Florida State; (7) Utah vs. Brigham Young; (8) California vs. Stanford; (9) Georgia vs. Florida; (10) Oregon vs. Oregon State.

Various factors make for rivalries. Often the games go way back—the Big Ten's Minnesota Golden Gophers and Wisconsin Badgers (who play for "Paul Bunyan's Axe") first battled in 1890, while the "Border War" between the Missouri Tigers and Kansas Jayhawks began one year later.

Geography often plays a role, too—as you can see from the names above, many of the rivals come from the same or neighboring states. But the competitiveness of the series adds to a rivalry's stature: in the case of those 120-year-plus Minnesota/Wisconsin and Missouri/Kansas series, no more than three victories separate the teams.

Rivalries generate excitement, but sometimes bad blood, too. The apostle Paul found that in his ministry when other preachers questioned his calling and results. "It is true that some preach Christ out of envy and rivalry," Paul wrote to the Philippians (1:15). But even though God forbids such things, He can still—in His amazing power and wisdom—use rivalry for His good purposes. "What does it matter?" Paul asked. "The important thing is that in every way, whether from false motives or true, Christ is preached" (Philippians 1:18).

And we know that in all things God works for the good of those who love him, who have been called according to his purpose.
ROMANS 8:28

HOLDING ON TO HOPE

Letting go of a dream is no easy task. Sometimes it's necessary, but sometimes it's better to hold on to hope.

Kurt Warner was eligible for the NFL Draft in 1994, but no teams came calling. He was signed as an undrafted free agent by Green Bay, then sent home. A third-string quarterback at the University of Northern Iowa until his final year in college, it seemed he didn't have what it took to impress the NFL.

So he turned to stocking shelves at a local grocery store. Without interest from the NFL, Warner turned to the Arena Football League in 1995. He built a very successful career that placed him in that league's Hall of Fame.

In time, the NFL took notice. The St. Louis Rams signed Warner in 1998 and promptly sent him to its European league. There he more than proved his capabilities as a quarterback. Warner returned to the Rams as a third-string quarterback, but the following year got a starting nod when quarterback Trent Green was injured. By year's end, Warner was named the NFL's Most Valuable Player.

Warner also played for the New York Giants and the Arizona Cardinals, retiring after the 2009 season with a Super Bowl win and a list of awards, accomplishments, and accolades that would make a number one draft choice jealous. Warner achieved his success the hard way, dream intact.

We are never promised an easy life. We may not succeed in everything we do. But when hard times come, remember James 1:12: "Blessed is the one who perseveres under trial because, having stood the test, that person will receive the crown of life that the Lord has promised to those who love him."

The end result of all the hard work is hope.

We also glory in our sufferings, because we know that suffering produces perseverance; perseverance, character; and character, hope.
ROMANS 5:3–4

EXAMINING ANOTHER MAN'S SHOES

Terry Bradshaw is a football analyst who brings recognizable humor to his job. While many have appreciated his humor through the years, there was a time when Bradshaw was laughed at for his rural leanings.

Born in Shreveport, Louisiana, Bradshaw would be a standout quarterback at Louisiana Tech. In 1970 he would be taken first in the draft by the Pittsburgh Steelers. It took nearly four seasons for Bradshaw to adjust to playing in the NFL, but once he did, he would lead his team to four Super Bowl titles in six years. This accomplishment was unprecedented.

In spite of his successes, Bradshaw was publicly heckled by Thomas "Hollywood" Henderson of the Dallas Cowboys prior to their meeting in Super Bowl XIII: "[Bradshaw] couldn't spell 'cat' if you spotted him the 'c' and the 'a.' " Bradshaw responded by winning the game and being named MVP. The accolades would continue, culminating in his admittance to the Hall of Fame.

In time the public would learn that Bradshaw suffered anxiety attacks, depression, and sleeplessness. He struggled enough that his condition prevented him from attending the funeral of Steelers owner Art Rooney.

Bradshaw's rough-and-tumble game play may be responsible for short-term memory loss. As much as football is a crowd-influenced sport, Bradshaw now feels most comfortable in the controlled atmosphere of the studio—away from the crowd.

It can be easy to criticize anyone for the slightest reason. It is much easier to kick than help when a person is down, but Colossians 3:12 says, "Clothe yourselves with compassion, kindness, humility, gentleness and patience."

No one has to be perfect to be kind. You can respond with compassion whether you feel like it or not. You get to choose your response.

> *Finally, all of you, be like-minded, be sympathetic,*
> *love one another, be compassionate and humble.*
> 1 PETER 3:8

KEEP HOME IN MIND

Here's an odd bit of sports history: no NFL team has ever played host to a Super Bowl in its own stadium. Said another way, no team has been able to go home to finish its season as Super Bowl champion.

This is known as the Super Bowl Curse, and it means that if the Super Bowl is held at your team's stadium, you can count on your team failing to make the Big Game that season. In recent years, most host teams have not even qualified for the playoffs. This has been true for every year of the 2000s except 2000 and 2014. In 2000, the Tampa Bay Buccaneers qualified for the playoffs but fell short of the Big Game. In 2014, the Arizona Cardinals also made the playoffs but lost their wild card matchup against the Carolina Panthers.

A story in the Minneapolis Star-Tribune acknowledged the potency of the curse and stated that the Vikings, who have gone 0–4 in the Big Game, would need "good luck" to win the 2018 Super Bowl in their new stadium.

A football team longs to play as many home games as possible. That longing can translate into wanting to host the Super Bowl. Curse or no curse, to eagerly await a home game is only natural.

Christians tend to live like NFL teams in that they never get to play the big game on their home turf. Home is not tied to this planet. Home is a place called heaven. That is where God dwells. In that sense, it is the greater home, the one that is anticipated.

Believers are citizens of this God locality. He rests there (see John 14:2), and we will, too. But for now, it is evident that we are unable to play the Super Bowl in that place. Our challenge, then, is to take what we know about it and experience its future blessings by faith.

But our citizenship is in heaven.
And we eagerly await a Savior from there, the Lord Jesus Christ.
PHILIPPIANS 3:20

UNSTOPPABLE EXPANSION

The NFL has expanded several times since merging with the American Football League in 1970. The Tampa Bay Buccaneers and Seattle Seahawks were added in 1976. The Carolina Panthers and Jacksonville Jaguars joined in 1995. And the Houston Texans are the league's newest team, joining in 2002. The Baltimore Ravens, who began operations in 1996, were founded when then–Cleveland Browns owner Art Modell moved his franchise from Cleveland to Baltimore.

The league currently stands at thirty-two teams. The sports world has been talking about the possibility of the league expanding again. London continues to be mentioned as a possible option. But Commissioner Roger Goodell says the league isn't currently focused on expansion.

A number of key factors come into play when expansion is considered, including the support of local leaders, procurement of a financially viable owner, a suitably large population to support a team, sufficient public tolerance for construction and/or a tax hike, a logical way to restructure current divisions, and numerous other items.

When the kingdom of God expands, no such concerns arise. In the days following Pentecost, new converts devoted themselves daily to the apostles' teaching, the breaking of bread, prayer, and fellowship. "They broke bread in their homes and ate together with glad and sincere hearts, praising God and enjoying the favor of all the people. And the Lord added to their number daily those who were being saved" (Acts 2:46–47).

"The kingdom of heaven is like a mustard seed, which a man took and planted in his field. Though it is the smallest of all seeds, yet when it grows, it is the largest of garden plants and becomes a tree."
Matthew 13:31–32

A SPECIAL CHRISTMAS TRADITION

At Christmas 2013, then-Houston Texans All-Pro wide receiver Andre Johnson continued a tradition he had begun seven years earlier. Johnson invited a dozen children in the care of child protective services to join him at a Toys "R" Us store, giving each one 80 seconds to pick out whatever they wanted. Why 80 seconds? Johnson's uniform number is 80.

Each of the kids was assisted by a Houston cheerleader. A video of the event shows happy children piling their carts full—many with toys and gadgets for their siblings as well.

"I got a lot of Barbie stuff, because I like Barbies," one girl says. "And I had a lot of fun because I had a cheerleader and she was helping me with everything."

"It's a great time," Johnson says in the video. "You get a chance to just give back to the community. I remember as a little kid I wasn't able to get things that I wanted for Christmas, so you just give these a kids a chance to go out and get what they want for Christmas. That's pretty much why I do it."

In so doing, Andre Johnson is practicing Jesus' teaching in Matthew 7:12, which many call the Golden Rule: "Do to others what you would have them do to you."

In addition to everything the children grabbed, Johnson also bought each one a gaming console and two games. His total bill for the day? According to *USA Today*, it was $17,352.

You don't have to spend in the five figures to bless a child at Christmastime. You might not spend anything. . .and it could be any day of the year. The only rule is golden: Do what you'd like others to do for you.

Religion that God our Father accepts as pure and faultless is this:
to look after orphans and widows in their distress.
JAMES 1:27

WHAT'S IN A NAME?

Sportswriters earn a living describing games and players. Sometimes their more clever descriptions stand the test of time.

Chicago Daily News sportswriter Francis Powers once wrote that Elroy Hirsch's "crazy legs were gyrating in six different directions, all at the same time; he looked like a demented duck." Many people agreed, and stopped using the name Elroy. "Crazylegs Hirsch" stuck.

A receiver for the Los Angeles Rams in the early 1950s, Hirsch didn't run like anyone else. But he still managed to chew up yards like a child plowing through a bag of Gummi Bears. He helped the Rams reach three NFL championship games, winning it all in 1951.

In 1968, eleven years after his final pro game, Hirsch was elected to Pro Football's Hall of Fame. A modest man, Hirsch would say, "I'm just a busted-down, retreaded halfback who happened to get lucky."

This busted-down halfback would later take his skills back to his home state, where, as athletic director for the University of Wisconsin, he helped to build a premier college football program with the Badgers. His nickname is still associated with an annual benefit run for Wisconsin athletics: the Crazylegs Classic.

New names are something God gives, too. When He saves us, He changes our names. No longer are we called "Liar," "Cheat," or "Sinner." We get the new name "Friend of God." In John 15:15 Jesus says, "I no longer call you servants, because a servant does not know his master's business. Instead, I have called you friends, for everything that I learned from my Father I have made known to you."

That's a new name that will stand the test of time—for all time.

*"To the one who is victorious, I will give some of the hidden manna.
I will also give that person a white stone with a new name
written on it, known only to the one who receives it."*
REVELATION 2:17

MANIACS ARE OKAY

Playing football like a maniac does not necessarily build a good reputation. Is it nice to be called wildly insane? You make the call.

If a football player were to attempt this, perhaps the best place to do so would be the linebacker position. Do lunatics play there? Maybe. Are there raving, rabid dogs playing in the middle of a 4–3 defense or on the inside of a 5–2? If so, would it be proper and Christian to call these human beings maniacs?

One candidate for maniac status is James Laurinaitis. He has earned this reputation as a middle linebacker with the St. Louis Rams, and his bloodlines are dripping with insanity from top to bottom. His father, Joe, wrestled professionally under the name "Animal" as part of the "Road Warriors" tag team. He also has two uncles (Johnny Ace and The Terminator) who wrestled.

The stereotype of maniacs is that they all lack smarts and are full of lunacy. Laurinaitis bucks the stereotype in that he was a three-time All-American linebacker for Ohio State University who won numerous awards (Butkus, Nagurski, and Lott, to name a few). As maniacs go, he does have credentials.

Maniacs are going to have tribulation in the world (see John 16:33). Jesus told us that. If you are a maniac, in Christ, with the Holy Spirit living inside of you, clean by the blood of Yeshua, be encouraged. Jesus loves you (John 16:33 again; look it up).

"It's a good feeling if you're actually able to sit down and comprehend what He's saying," Laurinaitis said. "I think that all Christians can kind of just rest in that."

Jehu drove like a maniac. Jehu was a king. Did God love Jehu? You make the call.

> *The lookout reported, "He has reached them, but he isn't coming back either. The driving is like that of Jehu son of Nimshi—he drives like a maniac."*
> 2 Kings 9:20

OFF TO THE RACES

To get to the NFL, Renaldo Nehemiah took an unusual track.

Nehemiah was a track star, the world record holder in the 110-meter hurdles and favorite to win gold at the 1980 Summer Olympics. He never got a chance to compete, though, when the United States boycotted those games in Moscow.

Though he had not played football in college (at the University of Maryland), Nehemiah intrigued several NFL teams. He worked out with the Cowboys, Patriots, Giants, Eagles, Steelers, 49ers, and Redskins in 1982, ultimately signing with San Francisco as a wide receiver. But if 49ers officials hoped Nehemiah's speed and jumping ability would lead to lots of scoring, they would be disappointed—in three seasons, the former track star appeared in forty games, recording 43 catches and four touchdowns.

Some felt Nehemiah dropped too many passes during his short NFL tenure. But Nehemiah himself thought his coach, Bill Walsh, was too protective of him, especially after the 6'1", 180-pound speedster was knocked unconscious in 1983 by Falcons defensive back Kenny Johnson.

Whatever his limitations as a player, Nehemiah's brief NFL career included the ultimate team achievement. On January 21, 1985, his 49ers, behind quarterback Joe Montana, defeated the Dolphins in Super Bowl XIX. The world-class runner had earned the famed prize of football success, "the ring."

Using a footrace as an analogy for the Christian life, the apostle Paul urged believers to pursue a much greater prize—the "crown that will last forever" (1 Corinthians 9:25). "Do you not know that in a race all the runners run, but only one gets the prize?" Paul asked. "Run in such a way as to get the prize" (1 Corinthians 9:24).

For believers, the race of life allows for no dawdling, no detours, and no dropping out. It's not always easy, but perseverance leads to everlasting honor.

I do not run like someone running aimlessly.
1 CORINTHIANS 9:26

STANDING IN THE GAP

Former Minnesota Golden Gopher head coach Jerry Kill had been suffering with epileptic seizures since 2000. After he sought medical attention for one of them, doctors discovered he had developed stage 4 kidney cancer. Kill's wife, Rebecca, believes her husband's seizure on that particular day saved his life, because the cancer probably wouldn't have been discovered, and subsequently treated in time, otherwise.

Kill has made lifestyle changes, but the seizures still occur. During his time as head coach at Minnesota, he had at least four more on game days. After he experienced a seizure in 2012, one "fan" sent him an e-mail saying, "We've got a freak coaching the Minnesota Gophers." It made him wonder what life must be like for children with epilepsy. If a fan was willing to demean an epileptic coach, what sort of bullying must epileptic schoolchildren suffer? In that moment, he became an advocate.

"I'm not a freak, and neither are they. We're normal people," he said on his next weekly radio show. "And I'm going to work my tail end off for the people that have the same situation I have."

If he meets a parent who has a child with epilepsy, Kill gives that parent his cell phone number. He formed the Chasing Dreams fund to help pay for seizure-smart school initiatives as well as for a summer camp for children with epilepsy. He stands in the gap for those who need him.

In Ezekiel 22, we read of God's anger at the people of the land who weren't treating others with respect: "I looked for someone among them who would build up the wall and stand before me in the gap on behalf of the land so I would not have to destroy it, but I found no one" (verse 30).

The same cannot be said about Coach Kill.

Speak up for those who cannot speak for themselves,
for the rights of all who are destitute.
PROVERBS 31:8

SUFFERING NEED NOT BE IN VAIN

A young NFL wide receiver dreams about catching the winning touchdown pass in the Super Bowl. Sometimes it happens, but most of the time it doesn't. And then there is the story of Darryl Stingley.

Stingley knew suffering. In an August 12, 1978, preseason game, he attempted to catch a pass for the New England Patriots when Oakland Raiders safety Jack Tatum hit him hard, helmet to shoulder pad, breaking his neck and leaving him a quadriplegic for the rest of his life. He died in 2007 at the age of fifty-five from the medical complications tied to his injury.

Over the years, Stingley seemed to accept his hardships. In 1983, he coauthored a book titled *Happy to Be Alive*. And in 2003, when asked by the *Boston Globe* about Tatum having part of his leg amputated due to diabetes, Stingley said he rejected being hateful because "God teaches us to love."

It is intellectually dishonest to read the Bible apart from its doctrine on suffering, which is why the story of Darryl Stingley can be instructional. Suffering happens. Jesus said it plainly (see John 16:33), and the Bible offers it liberally. Consider how badly one man, the apostle Paul, was mistreated. His pain runs freely through the pages of the New Testament.

At one point, Paul described himself as being both hungry and thirsty as well as poorly clothed, beaten, and homeless (see 1 Corinthians 4:11). Once he was stoned and thought to be dead. And the lesson? We enter the kingdom of God through many tribulations (see Acts 14:22).

A fairy-tale ending in the Super Bowl may be nice, but Jesus suffered. He alone is able to transform pain into faith, hope, and love.

Three times I was beaten with rods, once I was pelted with stones,
three times I was shipwrecked, I spent a night and a day in the open sea.
2 CORINTHIANS 11:25

UNFULFILLED POTENTIAL

Okay, football fans. . .take a look at the following list and make a mental note of what they have in common: JaMarcus Russell, Ryan Leaf, Tony Mandarich, Tim Couch, Brian Bosworth, Charles Rogers, Andre Ware, Akili Smith, Ki-Jana Carter.

If you're a fan of the Oakland Raiders, San Diego Chargers, Green Bay Packers, or any of the other teams that gave these players a shot at playing in the NFL, you know the answer—and you likely cringe when you think about it.

All of these players were high—as high as number one overall—NFL Draft picks who, for various reasons, didn't pan out for the teams that selected them. Some of the players failed because of poor work habits, while others didn't play to their potential due to injuries. Still others didn't have the mental toughness it takes to make it in the NFL. And then there are those who came into the league believing that their talent alone would carry them to stardom.

Sometimes "can't-miss" draft prospects *do* miss, and when they do, they set back the progress of the teams that selected them—sometimes for several seasons in a row.

In a very real way, the same thing can happen when we don't make the best use of the gifts God has given us.

The Bible teaches that God, through the Holy Spirit, has given each follower of Christ a gift or a set of gifts and has called each of us to use those gifts for the glory of God and the good of others. But when we allow selfishness or apathy to crowd our hearts, we render His gifts useless.

For that reason, we should all follow this advice from the apostle Paul to a young preacher named Timothy: "For this reason I remind you to fan into flame the gift of God, which is in you" (2 Timothy 1:6).

Each of you should use whatever gift you have received to serve others,
as faithful stewards of God's grace in its various forms.
1 PETER 4:10

INSTALLING THE HEIDI PHONE

In November 1968, fans were glued to their television sets watching the Oakland Raiders battle the New York Jets. The score was close, the crowd was enthusiastic—and the game was running long.

It was shaping up to be a classic, with two of the American Football League's best teams locked in a seesaw battle. But NBC had been promoting a new production of the children's story *Heidi*, to begin exactly at 7:00 p.m.

While ten future Hall of Famers competed on-field, thousands of people called NBC to argue for either the completion of the game or the start of the movie. Dick Cline, an NBC programmer, awaited a call from network executives but never heard from them. As it turned out, NBC officials wanted to stay with the game but were unable to reach Cline because of all the viewer calls.

So at seven o'clock, with less than a minute remaining in the game, Cline transitioned to *Heidi*. And in that final minute of play—within nine seconds—Oakland scored *two* touchdowns for a 43–32 come-from-behind victory.

This incident changed the way networks handle NFL games. For one thing, the league's contract demanded that entire games be shown, at least in their home markets. And NBC installed a "Heidi phone" in the control room, a line dedicated for use in just such an emergency.

In the "Heidi Bowl," mistakes were made and tempers were stirred. But all of life has its Heidi Bowls—in our families, workplaces, and churches. What do we do when things get crazy? "Bear with each other and forgive one another if any of you has a grievance against someone. Forgive as the Lord forgave you" (Colossians 3:13).

That's God calling on your personal Heidi phone.

"But to you who are listening I say:
Love your enemies, do good to those who hate you."
Luke 6:27

MOURN WITH THOSE WHO MOURN

On September 28, 2013, Ohio State defeated Wisconsin 31–24. Eleven days earlier, Dom Tiberi, sports director at the CBS affiliate in Columbus, had lost his twenty-one-year-old daughter in a car accident.

As Buckeye players and personnel left their field of victory, they spotted Tiberi returning to his work—and reached out to him in an emotional show of support. Nearly everyone in Ohio State's program waited in line to embrace Tiberi. Some offered words of encouragement, while others let their hug do the talking. For nearly three minutes, players and staffers of differing races, sizes, and presumably beliefs mourned with a grieving father.

"Good to see you," one player said.

"I'm glad to be seen," Tiberi responded.

"Appreciate you," another player offered.

"God bless you," said a member of the staff.

One player hugged Tiberi so hard he nearly knocked off his headphones. When the long procession finally ended, Tiberi adjusted his headphones and tried to take in everything that had just happened. "Whoa," he said. "That was amazing." He let out a breath, dropped his head, and tried to keep his emotions in check. But who would have blamed him if he had broken down in tears?

The apostle Paul, in Romans 12:15, encouraged Christians to "mourn with those who mourn." We would hope that's a natural human instinct, but it never hurts to be reminded to stop and consider just what others are experiencing. Such compassion has a real impact on the suffering because it lets them know they are not alone in their grief. An old saying is true: "Grief shared is half grief; joy shared is double joy."

Sometimes football teams provide much more than just Saturday entertainment.

Carry each other's burdens,
and in this way you will fulfill the law of Christ.
GALATIANS 6:2

COLT MCCOY, QUARTERBACK

Born September 5, 1986, in Hobbs, New Mexico

Played for University of Texas Longhorns (2006–09)

First-team All-American (2008, 2009)

Heisman Trophy finalist, runner-up (2008)

Heisman Trophy finalist, third place (2009)

Third-round pick in NFL Draft by Cleveland Browns (2010)

Played for Browns (2010–12), 49ers (2013), Redskins (2014–)

6'1", 214 pounds, throws right

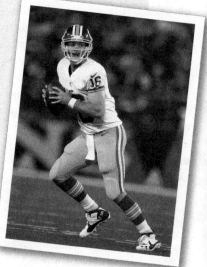

"I always give God the glory. I never question why things happen the way they do. God is in control of my life, and I know that. . .I am standing on the Rock." (from postgame comments after being injured early in 2010 BCS National Championship Game against Alabama)

THE HIGHER ROCK

In the mid-1960s, S.C. Jones, a Clemson alumnus, while on a trip to California, picked up a rock in Death Valley. Presbyterian College coach Lonnie McMillan had dubbed Clemson's Memorial Stadium "Death Valley" because he said his teams went there to die every year. Knowing that history, Jones brought the rock back as a gift for legendary coach Frank Howard.

The rock sat in Howard's office until 1966, when he asked a member of the booster club to "take this rock and throw it over the fence, or out in the ditch. . .do something with it, but get it out of my office!" The booster decided to mount the rock on a pedestal and had it placed above the east end zone before a game on September 24, 1966, against Virginia. The Tigers were down by 18 points near the end of the third quarter, but came back to win 40–35.

Coach Howard, looking to motivate his players the following season, told them, "If you're going to give me 110 percent, you can rub that rock. If you're not, keep your filthy hands off of it." Clemson players have been rubbing it before games ever since (with the exception of two and a half years in the early 1970s).

"Howard's Rock" doesn't contain any real power but is part of a beautiful tradition that honors a strong work ethic and all of the players and coaches who have gone before the current roster. Psalm 62:2, on the other hand, describes God as the all-powerful Rock: "Truly he is my rock and my salvation; he is my fortress, I will never be shaken."

From the ends of the earth I call to you, I call as my heart grows faint; lead me to the rock that is higher than I.
PSALM 61:2

LIVIN' AND PREACHIN'

When you think of longtime college football coach Paul "Bear" Bryant, it's hard to visualize him standing behind a pulpit, preaching the Gospel. Bryant is remembered—very fondly by folks in Tuscaloosa—as the architect of six national championships and thirteen conference titles with the Crimson Tide.

Bryant finished his thirty-eight-year career as a head coach (he also coached Maryland, Kentucky, and Texas A&M) with what was at the time of his 1982 retirement an NCAA record 323 wins. His accomplishments as a coach landed him in the College Football Hall of Fame.

But if Bear's mother had had her way, he never would have coached a single game, let alone become a college football legend. The way she saw it, God had a higher calling for her son. "Mama wanted me to be a preacher," Bryant once said. "I told her coachin' and preachin' were a lot alike."

While Bryant's personal life in some ways didn't reflect that of a preacher of the Gospel, there is some great biblical truth in his assertion that coaching and preaching have a lot in common. As a coach, Bryant worked to instill his values in the young men who played for him—just as a Christian minister does with his own "flock."

A follower of Christ should approach his or her life and work—no matter what it may be—as an opportunity to make Him known to others. In that respect, to paraphrase Bear, "livin' and preachin' are a lot alike."

God may not be calling you to preach or teach or travel to faraway lands to take the Gospel message to people. But He has called you to be His ambassador—no matter where you live and no matter what you do for a living.

"Let your light shine before others, that they may see your good deeds and glorify your Father in heaven."
MATTHEW 5:16

STRONGEST EVER

There's no definitive way to identify the best college football team of all time. . .but that doesn't stop many from offering their opinions.

Certain websites suggest the 1995 Nebraska Cornhuskers should be near if not at the very top of that list. ESPN.com ranks the Tom Osborne–coached team in third place of all time—after the 1971 Cornhuskers and the '72 USC Trojans. But BleacherReport.com calls the '95 Nebraska squad "quite simply, the most dominant team in college football history."

By finishing the 1995 season at 12–0, Nebraska recorded both a second straight perfect season (the '94 'Huskers had gone 13–0) and a second straight national championship. Averaging 53 points per game while giving up only 14, Osborne's boys won each game by an average of more than *five* touchdowns. They defeated four Top 10 teams, each by at least 23 points. Nebraska trailed only once all year, and whipped previously undefeated Florida 62–24 in the season-ending Fiesta Bowl. Factor in all the variables, and the 1995 'Huskers may be the strongest team ever.

There's no "maybe" when it comes to the power of God. The most powerful people in the world pale in comparison, as King Nebuchadnezzar of Babylon learned—the hard way. Disregarding the warning of Daniel, who had interpreted a disturbing dream of the king, Nebuchadnezzar boasted of his own power and was immediately humbled by God. For seven years, the king lived like an animal, separated from his people (see Daniel 4:1–33).

When he finally regained his senses, Nebuchadnezzar honored God by testifying, "He does as he pleases with the powers of heaven and the peoples of the earth. No one can hold back his hand or say to him: 'What have you done?'" (Daniel 4:35).

And how exciting for Christians—He's on our side!

> *God hath spoken once; twice have I heard this;*
> *that power belongeth unto God.*
> PSALM 62:11 KJV

THE GREATEST GAME

It was late December of 1958, and "the greatest game ever played" was keeping statisticians busy.

The Baltimore Colts faced the New York Giants in the twenty-sixth NFL championship game. Entering the game, both teams had 9–3 season records. Recent history indicated the Giants should have won. They had five consecutive winning seasons and had also defeated the Colts earlier in the season. But at the end of regulation the score was 17–17. For the first time in NFL history, a game would be determined in overtime.

Baltimore's Alan Ameche, known as the "Iron Horse," was a Heisman Trophy winner who had scored one of the Colts' touchdowns in the second quarter. Now in overtime, he bulled in for the game-winning one-yard score, making champions of himself, head coach Weeb Ewbank, and teammates like Johnny Unitas, Gino Marchetti, and Raymond Berry. Seventeen players and coaches on the field that day would eventually be inducted into the Hall of Fame.

This "greatest game" introduced several important new elements to professional football. In addition to the overtime period, some credit Unitas with initiating the two-minute drill. And many believe that the American Football League, which began the next year, was an outgrowth of the popularity of this single game, watched on television by more than forty-five million people.

Someday, God will make *all* things new for His children. He won't just tweak or add to this life; He'll change it completely. No longer will we experience sadness, pain, or death, "for the old order of things has passed away. . . . I am making everything new!" (Revelation 21:4–5).

At that point, every loss will be forgotten. Eternity will be nothing but victories.

You make known to me the path of life; you will fill me with joy
in your presence, with eternal pleasures at your right hand.
PSALM 16:11

INSPIRED BY A DEER

Graceful, agile, swift in the open field, deer can be hard to catch. The same holds true for some football players.

Charlie Flowers took a look at his San Diego Chargers teammate, Lance Alworth, and nicknamed him after the movie deer Bambi. Alworth said the nickname arose because he had "a little short flattop and big brown eyes and I ran with my knees really high." He didn't care for the moniker, but others seemed to think it fit. From 1962 through 1972, Bambi Alworth put together a Hall of Fame career.

One leader of the twelve tribes of Israel, Naphtali, was called a deer by his father. But as the elderly Jacob pronounced blessings on his sons, he didn't identify Naphtali as a majestic buck. No, Jacob said, "Naphtali is a doe set free that bears beautiful fawns" (Genesis 49:21).

Back to the football field, Lance Alworth—with his athletic jumping and artful running after catches—was a dynamic symbol of the old American Football League. And while Alworth was tagged with one of the more disarming nicknames in sports history, he does have something on Naphtali. At least Bambi is male.

It may not seem terribly manly to be called "Bambi," but the gentle, graceful deer is used in the Bible to teach and inspire. "As the deer pants for streams of water," the psalmist wrote, "so my soul pants for you, my God" (Psalm 42:1). In a song written after military successes, David said, "It is God who arms me with strength. . . . He makes my feet like the feet of a deer; he causes me to stand on the heights" (2 Samuel 22:33–34).

So Naphtali, the "doe," is set free to take his place in history. The wall of the New Jerusalem will feature his name! That's manly enough.

On the gates were written the names of the twelve tribes of Israel.
Revelation 21:12

A FATHER TO THE FATHERLESS

Imagine the pain a ten-year-old girl must feel when her elementary school plans a father-daughter dance. . .but her father is gone, a victim of brain cancer two years earlier.

That's the situation young Nadia Marotti, a Chicago Bears fan, found herself in. But Chicago defensive tackle Nate Collins stepped in as a surrogate father for the dance. He learned about Nadia's situation when her mother sought items for a benefit auction for an organization called Voices Against Brain Cancer. Collins offered to stand in for Nadia's father, and she accepted. He picked the girl up in a black limousine.

The 6'2", 279-pounder was scheduled to host a draft party that May day in 2014, but opted to go to Nadia's dance instead.

"This is way more important and I know how much fun Nadia is going to have tonight and how much it means to this family," Collins told a local newspaper reporter. "It was a great opportunity to jump in."

In so doing, Nate Collins became a "father to the fatherless," giving football fans—and everyone else—a beautiful hint of God in heaven, as described in Psalm 68:5: "A father to the fatherless, a defender of widows, is God in his holy dwelling."

Nate Collins was released by the Bears at the beginning of the 2014 season. No matter where he ends up, though, he can be proud of filling a void in a little girl's heart, creating a memory she'll never forget.

Look around you. Are there any lonely children nearby whom you can serve in a similar way?

But you, God, see the trouble of the afflicted; you consider their grief
and take it in hand. The victims commit themselves to you;
you are the helper of the fatherless.
PSALM 10:14

POSITION TRANSITION

Byron "Whizzer" White had a career with the University of Colorado that almost included a Heisman Trophy. In 1937, he placed second in balloting to Yale halfback Clint Frank.

The NFL's Pittsburgh Pirates (later the Steelers) made White a first-round draft pick in 1938. Two years later, he transitioned to the Detroit Lions. Before long, White was one of the league's highest-paid players at $15,000 a year.

He was worth the money. White was the NFL's leading rusher in 1938 and 1940, and an All-Pro each of his three seasons. But just as his successes mounted, war came knocking. White answered by joining the Navy in 1941. When he came home, he chose not to return to pro football. His new career course took him to Yale Law School, where he earned high honors.

This change led eventually to his appointment to the US Supreme Court by President John F. Kennedy. White lent his expertise to rulings that affected American law for more than three decades.

Like Whizzer White, we can't always control our circumstances—but we can choose how we respond to them. We can become frustrated by needed course corrections. We could be bitter at the loss of a dream. We might even struggle for readmittance to our old life. But for those who love God, even better things lie ahead.

"You were taught, with regard to your former way of life," the apostle Paul said, "to put off your old self, which is being corrupted by its deceitful desires; to be made new in the attitude of your minds; and to put on the new self, created to be like God in true righteousness and holiness" (Ephesians 4:22–24).

That's a position transition with eternal benefits.

Trust in the LORD with all your heart and lean not on your own
understanding; in all your ways submit to him,
and he will make your paths straight.
PROVERBS 3:5–6

ACCEPT, ADAPT, ADJUST, ADVANCE

When it comes to the most games played by a single NFL player, the current top spot goes to former multi-team quarterback Brett Favre. He played for 291 games before retiring in 2010, but even he said, "I may be a successful football player, but I feel like such a failure."

Barry Sanders set a multitude of records with the Detroit Lions. Most believe he could have played a lot longer, but in the end he suggested, "I don't know the right way to retire."

Former Miami Dolphins quarterback Dan Marino is recalled as one of the greatest players in the history of the NFL. He set multiple records and signed large contracts to play, but in the end he said, "Sometimes, I wish we were all amateurs again. I'd play for nothing. Ab-so-lute-ly free. But that's not the system."

Former San Francisco 49ers quarterback Joe Montana looked back on his time on the gridiron and said, "I miss the game—I miss it a lot."

"Broadway" Joe Namath was a flamboyant quarterback for the New York Jets. He was positive, and his actions were infectious. Yet he once said, "I was a very naive young man, and I may still be ignorant about a lot of things."

The Bible records the words of a man who played with the best and had plenty of personal accolades, but expressed the same life dissatisfaction. King Solomon, the wisest man who ever lived, said in Ecclesiastes 1:2, "'Meaningless! Meaningless!' says the Teacher. 'Utterly meaningless! Everything is meaningless.'"

While these NFL players said many more *positive* things, we sense their relatable struggle with life change. But such changes don't have to leave us feeling as if we're permanently benched. God will *never* forget us.

The plans of the LORD stand firm forever,
the purposes of his heart through all generations.
PSALM 33:11

A GOOD NAME

One of the best ambassadors for Jesus Christ in NFL history was a Hall of Fame coach named Thomas Wade Landry.

For twenty-nine seasons, Landry led the Dallas Cowboys with excellence while representing his Savior with class, dignity, and proper attire. He helped form the brand of "America's Team" as a stoic architect who wore a fedora and a conservative business suit, and his teams made it to five Super Bowls, winning two. During this era, the Cowboys enjoyed twenty consecutive winning seasons and an overall record of 270–178–6, ranking Landry third overall in career coaching victories.

When Landry died in 2000, evangelist Billy Graham described him as "one of the greatest Christian gentlemen I ever knew." Unbelievers talked about Landry's piety, which is defined as devotion to one's religious duties. Inscribed on the great coach's tombstone was Matthew 25:21, crediting him for a job well done as a good and faithful servant.

Tom Landry is a good name, maybe the best in all of pro football. Based on his body of work with the Fellowship of Christian Athletes, his reputation for football innovation (which mirrors the creative genius of God), and the peace he so reliably possessed for decades in a rugged sport, it could be argued that Landry was, and is, the gold standard for all things Christian in the pro game.

Roger Staubach, one of the more prominent Cowboys quarterbacks in the Landry era, spoke of the coach's impact at his funeral: "He was our rock, our hope, our inspiration. He was our coach. Probably there were some players that didn't love him, but they all respected him. He was committed to us, and you don't find that type of commitment in life very often."

Let the good name live on.

A good name is more desirable than great riches;
to be esteemed is better than silver or gold.
PROVERBS 22:1

COMPELLED TO SHARE

Ed Sabol never played a down in the NFL, but he revolutionized the way we watch the game today. As a result, at the age of ninety-four, he was inducted into the Hall of Fame in 2011.

Sabol was an aspiring filmmaker who had taken much more practical work selling overcoats for his father-in-law. But at the age of forty-five, he took a chance and contacted Commissioner Pete Rozelle about the rights to film the 1962 NFL championship game. After getting and shooting the gig in a venture that eventually became what we now know as NFL Films, he went on to use multiple cameras—adding one on the sideline to capture the players' emotions. He also put microphones on gridiron participants as well as introducing reverse-angle replay. And he came up with the idea for blooper footage. Fans have been benefiting ever since.

Sabol served as the president of NFL Films until 1985. His son, Steve, took over after he stepped down from the position. During the elder Sabol's tenure, NFL Films won fifty-two Emmy Awards, and deservedly so. He had a passion and drive for taking the game, in all its glory, to the masses.

As Christians, we have an even stronger passion for taking the Gospel to the masses. In fact, the apostle Paul said he *had* to preach the Gospel: "For when I preach the gospel, I cannot boast, since I am compelled to preach. Woe to me if I do not preach the gospel!" (1 Corinthians 9:16).

At daybreak, Jesus went out to a solitary place. The people were looking for him and when they came to where he was, they tried to keep him from leaving them. But he said, "I must proclaim the good news of the kingdom of God to the other towns also, because that is why I was sent."
Luke 4:42–43

SEEK AND DESTROY PRIDE

On the surface, what happened during an NFL playoff game at Lambeau Field on January 4, 2004, shows how pride can bring a player low. In truth, it may have been the voice of trash talk mimicking pride.

As the Seattle Seahawks and Green Bay Packers met at midfield for an overtime coin flip, Seahawks quarterback Matt Hasselbeck correctly called heads and said through the referee's microphone, "We want the ball, and we're gonna score." The opposite then happened, as Green Bay returned an interception for the game-winning touchdown.

The image of what Hasselbeck did in overtime plays well into the pride narrative. After throwing the interception, he dove at Packers cornerback Al Harris and failed to make a game-saving tackle. He was the last man brought low in defeat, and his words became a target for many to blast holes through.

Over the years, Hasselbeck has told a different story. His words, he has said, were meant to poke fun at former teammates. All he meant to do was engage in a little trash talk with good friends. He also hoped his words would motivate his young teammates, who likely doubted their ability to win.

"It was funny," Hasselbeck said. "It is what it is. My only regret is that we didn't score."

The line between an NFL player "talking trash" and expressing pride would appear to be thin. Judging when a joke turns into an offense is difficult. Jesus Himself put pride and foolishness together on a list of sins (Mark 7:22 NLT). Fun is not foolishness; confidence is not pride.

But pride can be a cruel customer.

Pride is alive (1 John 2:16). Like a venomous or constrictor snake, it seeks to kill you. Be humble then. Be humble and learn to mortify your pride. To mortify is to kill the sin that is seeking to kill you. Mortify your pride.

Pride brings a person low, but the lowly in spirit gain honor.
PROVERBS 29:23

BE CONTENT WHERE YOU ARE

The year was 1993. Unrestricted free agency had come to the NFL, and the first big prize was a defensive end named Reggie White.

Typically, free agents want big money, a large market, and a good team. White was leaving the Philadelphia Eagles and was strongly considering the Washington Redskins and San Francisco 49ers. As a Christian, he said he wanted to be in an urban area where he could do inner-city ministry. One more thing: God would tell him where to go, White said.

The Green Bay Packers wanted him, but all they really had was money. Green Bay is the smallest NFL market. It has no urban core. But it does have a sense of humor.

"Reggie," spoke Packers coach Mike Holmgren into White's answering machine. "This is God. Come to Green Bay."

Amazingly, White did. He took $17 million for four seasons, and good things started to happen. The Packers won Super Bowl XXXI, with Reggie recording three quarterback sacks. After retirement, he entered the Hall of Fame as a three-time NFL Defensive Player of the Year who was elected to thirteen consecutive Pro Bowls.

An ordained Baptist minister from the age of seventeen, White played for Jesus on the football field and carried the nickname the "Minister of Defense." He was known for both his Christian charity and his bold preaching. In retirement, he spent many hours studying the original Hebrew language of the Bible. He died in 2004 at the age of forty-three.

White learned to be content in Green Bay. Out of that came great gain not only for the littlest NFL franchise, but also for the kingdom of God. Any ministry that White may have felt he was losing was returned to him in the form of a stronger and surer platform.

Never underestimate the power of contentment.

But godliness with contentment is great gain.
1 Timothy 6:6

SUFFERING FOR A GREATER GOOD

Hall of Fame running back Walter Payton has a long and distinguished list of gridiron accomplishments to his name. Start with 16,726 yards rushing—at one time the NFL record. Then there are the 125 touchdowns (110 rushing and 15 receiving) and 21,803 all-purpose yards. The list goes on, of course, but one of his records is often overlooked (comparatively) and will almost certainly never be surpassed.

"Sweetness" started an NFL record (for running backs) 170 regular-season games and eight playoff games for 178 straight starts. Over his thirteen-year career, he missed just one game—during his rookie season.

To get an idea of just how amazingly durable Payton was, consider this: as an NFL running back, every time he touched the ball (more than 4,300 times, rushing and receiving), he was a target.

Some observers would say that Payton was just plain lucky to avoid injury. But it's hard to overlook his work ethic. His off-season workouts were the stuff of legend. He lifted weights every day, and he also ran gut-busting 65-yard courses in a sandbank by the Pearl River, near his hometown in Columbia, Mississippi. Not only that, but he intentionally did his running during the hottest time of the day.

Walter Payton made himself suffer so that he could be one of the greatest players in NFL history. "You get to a point where you have to keep pushing yourself. You stop, throw up, and push yourself again," he once said.

Most of us have no legitimate reason to intentionally put ourselves through suffering. But the simple truth is that suffering is often a part of life. We can take heart in clinging to the Bible's promise that God uses everything we go through to glorify Himself and to make us the kind of people He wants us to be.

We also glory in our sufferings, because we know that suffering produces perseverance; perseverance, character; and character, hope.
ROMANS 5:3–4

AN UNDESERVED GIFT

At age eleven, William "The Refrigerator" Perry weighed 200 pounds. "Even when I was little, I was big," he liked to say. A college teammate provided Perry's nickname, saying he was about the size of a large kitchen appliance.

But he was also athletic. In high school, Perry could dunk a basketball. He was the sixth fastest runner on his football team. He earned a full-ride scholarship to Clemson, playing on the Tigers' 1981 national championship team.

A first-round draft choice of the Chicago Bears in 1985, the 335-pound Perry was a crushing presence on defense but also occasionally on offense, scoring three touchdowns. Perry helped his team to a 15–1 record and a Super Bowl title.

But over the next few seasons, coaches criticized Perry for gaining too much weight. He was publicly called out for overeating, and even his wife was accused of serving him the wrong food. After a lackluster, ten-year NFL career ended, Perry struggled with both weight and alcoholism. And he was diagnosed with an immune system disorder called Guillain-Barré syndrome. The disease may be the reason Perry sold a valuable memento of his football career—his size 25 Super Bowl ring.

Here's where the story gets really interesting: A ten-year-old memorabilia collector named Cliff Forrest used his own college money to buy the ring. Then he sought out Perry and returned the ring as a gift. "I thought he needed it more than I did," Cliff said.

Such generosity reminds us of God's gift of salvation. His love, forgiveness, and favor are offered to us in spite of our many problems. As Romans 6:23 says, "The wages of sin is death, but the gift of God is eternal life in Christ Jesus our Lord." God offers us salvation not because we deserve it, but because we need it.

He saved us, not because of righteous things we had done,
but because of his mercy.
TITUS 3:5

THE DROPKICK

One of the quirks of the NFL rule book is that the dropkick is still legal.

A dropkick is just what its name implies. A player drops the football to the ground, and just as it bounces back upward, he kicks it—ideally, through the uprights. The key is to get the ball to bounce so that the foot can meet it squarely. The dropkick takes great skill—an ancient skill.

In the 1920s and '30s, the football was rounder. A dropkick was a weapon, and players often used it to score. But as the football grew pointier, the dropkick began to die off.

Ray "Scooter" McLean of the Bears converted the last dropkick, in a victory over the Giants for the NFL championship, on December 21, 1941. Well, the last one for sixty-five years, that is. It would have been the last step on an ancient path but for the historic sense of Patriots coach Bill Belichick.

Fast-forward to January 1, 2006. New England trails Miami in the fourth quarter. Belichick calls for a dropkick on an extra point. Backup quarterback Doug Flutie, at age forty-three playing his last NFL game, sets up in the shotgun formation, retreats to the 12-yard-line, and executes exactly what Belichick, a football historian, wants to see. The dropkick lives!

Dolphins coach Nick Saban was taken by surprise, but enjoyed the play. "I was kind of pleased to know that somebody can still dropkick," Saban said. "Thought it was a lost art."

The ancient Christian faith is a bit of a "lost art" in today's world. Why not revisit the old ways as found in God's Word? Joy is but a dropkick away.

This is what the LORD says: "Stand at the crossroads and look;
ask for the ancient paths, ask where the good way is, and walk in it,
and you will find rest for your souls."
JEREMIAH 6:16

TIM TEBOW, QUARTERBACK

Born August 14, 1987, in Makati, Philippines

University of Florida Gators (2006–09)

First-team All-American (2007, 2008)

Heisman Trophy winner (2007)

BCS National Championship (2007, 2009)

First-round pick in NFL Draft by Denver Broncos (2010)

Played for Broncos (2010–11), Jets (2012), Patriots (2013), Eagles (2015)

6'3", 245 pounds, throws left

"Dear Jesus, thank You for this day. Thank You for bringing together so many people that have a platform to influence people for You. Lord, as we disperse today, let us be united in love, hope, and peace. Lord, let us come together as one and break down all the barriers in between us that separate us. Lord, You came to seek and save that which is lost, and we thank You for that. Lord, we don't know what the future holds, but we know who holds the future, and in that there is peace, and in that there is comfort, and in that there is hope." (from closing prayer at 2010 National Prayer Breakfast)

NEVER TOO OLD

At the age of sixty-three, when most people are winding down in their careers, Dick LeBeau became the oldest rookie head coach since the AFL-NFL merger when he took over the helm of the Cincinnati Bengals in 2001.

After a long playing career with the Detroit Lions, the former cornerback, who went to the Pro Bowl three times, set his sights on becoming an NFL head coach. He always knew he wanted to be a head coach, but without any experience, his chances looked bleak. So he settled into a twenty-seven-year career as an assistant coach, serving in stints with the Philadelphia Eagles, the Green Bay Packers, the Pittsburgh Steelers, and the Bengals.

An article in the *Cincinnati Enquirer* says he coped with his disappointment at not landing a head job by feeding his intellect. The man who once played a stunt double in the World War II movie *Too Late the Hero* (1970) immersed himself in history books, biographies, and books about the Civil War. He also began visiting battlefields and other historical sites.

When the Bengals needed an interim head coach in 2000, LeBeau was happy to accept the position. He was named the new head coach the following season. His run in that position was short-lived, and he returned to assistant coaching. In fact, at the age of seventy-eight, he's still in the game as an associate head coach in charge of defense for the Tennessee Titans.

We are never too old for God to use us. He gave Abram the following instructions in Genesis 17:1–2: "When Abram was ninety-nine years old, the LORD appeared to him and said, 'I am God Almighty; walk before me faithfully and be blameless. Then I will make my covenant between me and you and will greatly increase your numbers.'"

The righteous will flourish like a palm tree. . . . They will still bear fruit in old age, they will stay fresh and green.
PSALM 92:12, 14

DEATH VISITS THE NFL

For an NFL wide receiver, Sunday is a time to shine. A time to go deep. A time to catch a short pass over the middle for a first down. A time to run a reverse. A time to dance in the end zone.

Then there are the familiar moments. The quarterback throws an incompletion. You jog back to the huddle. You die.

You die?

It happened on October 24, 1971, at Tiger Stadium in Detroit. The Detroit Lions were playing the Chicago Bears, and for Lions wide receiver Chuck Hughes, it was a time to die.

Hughes, twenty-eight, suffered a heart attack. He was later pronounced dead at a nearby hospital.

Death is when your body is separated from your soul. It happens once in your life, and it's by appointment (Hebrews 9:27). No one is exempt.

When it happens, the living will take it to heart (Ecclesiastes 7:2). The Bible describes death as both an enemy (1 Corinthians 15:26) and a terror (Hebrews 2:15). On earth, it can seem invincible. Even the young men of the NFL can be brought to a point where they acknowledge its power.

But death is not eternal.

Death, in fact, will end (1 Corinthians 15:54). As sure as an NFL scoreboard has a final reading, death has a final outcome. It will be swallowed up in victory. Right now it stings. It can strike you when you least expect it, and it can shock those who remain. But all of that is temporary. Death is not in charge.

Victory belongs to Christ (1 Corinthians 15:57). He was offered once on a cross to defeat death and bear your sins (Hebrews 9:28). Be blessed in your eternal victory as you eagerly wait for His return.

There is a time for everything, and a season for every activity under the heavens: a time to be born and a time to die.
ECCLESIASTES 3:1–2

DON'T LET THEM BEAT YOU TWICE

After an especially emotional—and unexpected—loss to a rival team, a college football coach addressed a sports reporter's question about how the team could bounce back the following Saturday.

"Well," the coach began, trying to gather his thoughts, "we have to do everything we can to make sure we don't let them beat us twice."

Though the coach's answer was one of countless sports clichés, it showed that he understood how a bitter loss had the potential to linger in his players' minds, affecting their performance in their next game.

If we're not careful, the same thing can happen to us in our walk with Christ.

Our opponent in the Christian life is the devil, and there are few things he loves more than putting stumbling blocks in our way, watching us trip over them, and then looking on gleefully as we allow that one stumble to keep us down for an extended period of time.

That is likely one of the reasons the apostle Peter wrote, "Be alert and of sober mind. Your enemy the devil prowls around like a roaring lion looking for someone to devour" (1 Peter 5:8). Peter knew about these things. After all, it was Peter who three times denied even knowing Jesus as He faced a trial that would result in His death on the Cross.

The good news is that Jesus later forgave and restored Peter, and the apostle went on to preach the world-shaking message of salvation through Christ.

When you fail, when you sin against your God, make sure you don't let the devil beat you twice. You may feel discouraged and disappointed in yourself, but you have a God who loves you and is ready and willing to forgive you, cleanse you of your sin, and set you back on the path He has for you.

If we confess our sins, he is faithful and just and will forgive us
our sins and purify us from all unrighteousness.
1 John 1:9

MODELING COMPASSION

Atlanta, Georgia, September 22, 2012. Miami Hurricanes quarterback Stephen Morris takes a three-step drop from the Georgia Tech 16-yard line and fires a missile to receiver Malcolm Lewis on a slant play over the middle. The Hurricanes are leading 12–0 and threatening to score again.

Lewis makes a 12-yard catch inside the five, but the Yellow Jacket defender ends up rolling over Lewis's left ankle, twisting it 180 degrees in a severe dislocation. Miami personnel rush to Lewis, who writhes in pain on the turf. Hurricanes head coach Al Golden, known for his intensity and under NCAA scrutiny for a possible recruiting violation, kneels down to cradle Lewis chest-to-chest as medical personnel tend to his injury. It's a gentle show of compassion from a coach who often displays forceful emotion on the sideline.

"That's what makes his moment of tenderness yesterday worth recognizing," said Timothy Burke in an article on Deadspin.com the day after the game. "Here's a coach whose career has been built on his identity as a tough guy, yet perhaps his career legacy (assuming he doesn't win a national championship) may be this touching episode."

Golden is no longer under investigation, and the Hurricanes finished 7–5 and 9–4 in 2012 and 2013, respectively. Still, Burke may be right about Golden's legacy. Winning is one way to build a name, but showing compassion is, too.

Even the non-religious recognize Jesus as a model of compassion. When Mary approached Jesus and fell at his feet in grief over the death of her brother, Lazarus, "Jesus saw her weeping, and the Jews who had come along with her also weeping, [and] he was deeply moved in spirit and troubled" (John 11:33).

What would Jesus do to show compassion? The Bible gives us many examples. What would you do?

Therefore, as God's chosen people, holy and dearly loved,
clothe yourselves with compassion, kindness,
humility, gentleness and patience.
Colossians 3:12

SOMETIMES YOU JUST GOTTA MOVE

Some players spend their entire professional career with one team. That wasn't quarterback Doug Flutie's experience.

After a stellar career at Boston College (in which he won the 1984 Heisman Trophy), Flutie awaited a call from the NFL. But when the Los Angeles Rams finally did call, 284 other players had already been drafted. Flutie decided to play for the New Jersey Generals of an NFL competitor, the United States Football League. The next year he was with the Chicago Bears, and two seasons later he joined the New England Patriots. But Flutie played only twenty-two NFL games in five years, and in 1990 jumped to the Canadian Football League. Here he would win three Grey Cup victories and earn six honors as the league's Most Outstanding Player.

In 1998 Flutie returned stateside to play for Buffalo. He would help the Bills to the playoffs and win both Pro Bowl and Comeback Player of the Year honors. Before retiring in 2005, Flutie would also play for the Chargers and return to the Patriots.

Why did he move so much? Flutie was known for his on-field scrambling in addition to the many career moves he made. Perhaps both relate to his height—Flutie is only 5'10" tall. "A guy that's undersized has to prove himself right away," Flutie said. Since he had God-given talents, worked hard, and was willing to go wherever he could contribute, he achieved much.

You can be a contributor, too, in whatever role God has for you. He wants your skill set. He knows where you fit. But you may have to go to wherever God is working. As Matthew 6:33 says, "Seek first his kingdom and his righteousness, and all these things will be given to you as well."

Being confident of this, that he who began a good work in you will carry it on to completion until the day of Christ Jesus.
PHILIPPIANS 1:6

THE LIFE OF A REDSHIRT FRESHMAN

If you are any kind of college football fan, you know that many—if not most—of the incoming freshmen on your favorite team don't become immediate stars. With few exceptions, freshmen play spot duty, help out on special teams, or sit out the entire season as a redshirt.

The redshirts spend their first season in college working out with the team, learning the team's system, helping in practice on the practice squad, and waiting for their shot.

Starting off a college career as a redshirt doesn't mean a player is sentenced to sitting on the bench for another four years. Far from it! Some players redshirt because they aren't quite ready to play college football, where the players are far bigger, far faster, and far more skilled than the ones they faced in high school. Still others redshirt because there are established players ahead of them.

In recent seasons, quarterbacks Johnny Manziel of Texas A&M, Marcus Mariota of Oregon, and Jameis Winston of Florida State all started off as redshirt freshmen—and they all wound up not just playing, but starring for their college teams and earning the Heisman Trophy.

Other than working out to get bigger and stronger, one of the most important jobs for a redshirt freshman is taking advantage of practice time so that he can show his coaches what he's capable of doing. Players who take good advantage of these opportunities earn their coaches' trust—little by little.

In some ways, God wisely and lovingly brings those of us who follow Him along slowly, giving us the opportunity to learn and grow, before He gives us more responsibilities and opportunities to serve Him. Our part of that arrangement is to take advantage of His instruction and rearing (which He so often provides through other believers) and prepare ourselves for bigger things.

"His master replied, 'Well done, good and faithful servant!
You have been faithful with a few things; I will put
you in charge of many things.'"
MATTHEW 25:23

CALLED OUT FOR GOD'S GLORY

Here's something you would never see in an NFL or major college matchup—a quarterback switching teams at halftime of a game.

His Brandon Bulldogs junior varsity team was up 21–0 in the second quarter of a 2014 game against the Northwest Rankin Cougars when the Cougars quarterback got hurt. The Cougars didn't have a backup, so they tried several other players, without success. The Bulldogs had two quarterbacks, so Coach Brad Peterson told his starter, Mason Mathieu, that he would continue to play in the second half—for the other team, a rival.

Mathieu led the Cougars to two second-half touchdowns and they were knocking on the door for a third when time ran out. The Bulldogs won the game 46–14, and after the game, Coach Peterson said he was glad to see Mathieu perform well under the pressure.

Mathieu had a blast.

"When I went over there, I guess [my team] really didn't know what to think, but I told them I was planning on going there and we were going to score a couple times," Mathieu said. "[The Cougars are] a great group of guys. I mean I loved it. It was great."

Sometimes God calls us out of familiar surroundings so we can make an impact for His glory in foreign lands or foreign environments. That's what happened to Abram in Genesis 12:1–2: "The LORD had said to Abram, 'Go from your country, your people and your father's household to the land I will show you. I will make you into a great nation, and I will bless you.'"

As Jesus was walking beside the Sea of Galilee, he saw two brothers, Simon called Peter and his brother Andrew. They were casting a net into the lake, for they were fishermen. "Come, follow me," Jesus said, "and I will send you out to fish for people."
MATTHEW 4:18–19

LIKE FATHER, LIKE SON

A fundamental teaching in the Bible is the way God the Father relates to God the Son, and vice versa. Truths found in that one pure relationship are almost too deep for words.

God the Father sends God the Son to die for and redeem sinful man. God the Son obeys and love gets a human face. The Father guides the Son through His darkest hour. The Son has faith that love will prevail. The Father has peace. The Son has hope. Call it a rainbow or a mosaic. . .beautiful art.

It may be possible to reach into the world of professional football and find something of comparable worth. Consider the story of Jack and Jeff Kemp.

Both had eleven-year pro careers as NFL quarterbacks. Jack starred with the Buffalo Bills in the 1960s while Jeff played for four different NFL teams from 1981 to 1991. Jack died in 2009, but Jeff continues on as a Christian leader, ministering now for Family Life in Little Rock, Arkansas.

In 2014, Jeff wrote about how three NFL players on the eve of the Super Bowl were excellent examples of how sons should view their fathers. Those players were Russell Wilson and Richard Sherman of the Seattle Seahawks and Peyton Manning of the Denver Broncos. He connected their examples with the relationship between him and his father, whom he described as a civic servant and leader in the public square. "He and my mom loved and shaped me, as my wife and I have aimed to do with our four sons," Kemp wrote.

The Father loves the Son and has given all things to him (see John 3:35). How might that impact us?

"A son honors his father, and a slave his master. If I am a father, where is the honor due me? If I am a master, where is the respect due me?" says the LORD Almighty.
MALACHI 1:6

A MATTER OF PRIDE

Terrell Owens didn't invent the touchdown celebration. But he certainly took it to new levels.

Owens, a six-time Pro Bowl wide receiver, assembled a large portfolio of outrageous end zone antics during his impressive fifteen-year career. Once as a 49er, after scoring in Dallas, he ran back to midfield to strike a pose on the Cowboys' large star logo. Two years later, in a Monday Night Football game against Seattle, he pulled a Sharpie marker from his sock, autographed the ball, and handed it to his financial advisor. The man was sitting in an end zone luxury suite owned by Shawn Springs, the cornerback Owens had beaten on the play.

He is also known for mocking Baltimore Ravens linebacker Ray Lewis's pregame dance, borrowing a cheerleader's pom-poms for a quick post-touchdown routine, and using the football he'd caught like a pillow for a fake nap in the end zone.

Give this to Owens: He had panache. It's also probably safe to assume that he had a fair amount of pride. And Owens isn't alone in that. In recent years, it seems as if NFL players are celebrating virtually every play with some sort of look-at-me routine.

Pride might make the *SportsCenter* highlight reels, but it doesn't impress God. In fact, He hates it. The prophet Isaiah shared God's feelings on the matter: "The eyes of the arrogant will be humbled and human pride brought low" (2:11). And Proverbs 16:18 is familiar, if not always followed: "Pride goes before destruction, a haughty spirit before a fall."

Instead of elevating ourselves, Christians are called to be humble. Our job is to direct all glory to God. Since we are sinners saved solely by His grace, we have nothing to brag about in ourselves. In heaven's eyes, the humble attitude is worthy of celebration.

> *"For those who exalt themselves will be humbled,*
> *and those who humble themselves will be exalted."*
> Matthew 23:12

GETTING HIS KICKS

Jan Stenerud followed a winding path into football. . .and all the way to the Hall of Fame.

Born in Norway, Stenerud came to the United States for college. He attended Montana State on a scholarship—in ski jumping. Once, while casually kicking a football with fellow skiers, his talents were noticed—by the *basketball* coach. Ultimately, the lanky skier, who had been one of Norway's top soccer prospects, joined the Bobcat football squad for two seasons. Highlights included making a then-record 59-yard field goal, and missing a 113-yarder. No joke—Stenerud, who kicked from his own end zone, says the coach thought he'd get better results from his placekicker than his punter, who had struggled against the wind. The kick reached midfield.

A third-round selection of Kansas City in the 1966 AFL Draft, Stenerud would play 263 professional games. He kicked thirteen years for the Chiefs, four with Green Bay, and two more with Minnesota, scoring 1,699 career points—second in history at the time. In 1991, Stenerud became the first pure placekicker elected to the Hall of Fame.

At 6'2", 187 pounds, Stenerud wasn't a football brute. But he had a knack for kicking that generated over 100 points in seven seasons. . .and the first nine points in the Chiefs' Super Bowl IV victory. Call it a "gift"—like the special abilities God gives those who follow Christ.

"We have different gifts, according to the grace given to each of us," the apostle Paul wrote. "If your gift is. . .serving, then serve; if it is teaching, then teach; if it is to encourage, then give encouragement; if it is giving, then give generously; if it is to lead, do it diligently; if it is to show mercy, do it cheerfully" (Romans 12:6–8).

How are you using your gift?

Now you are the body of Christ, and each one of you is a part of it.
1 Corinthians 12:27

A LASTING LEGACY

If you were to watch a recording of one of the first games in American football history, you probably wouldn't recognize it as football. The history of American football can be traced back to the early to mid-1800s, but in the beginning, football was a violent, dangerous game that often looked more like a mob scene than an athletic competition.

But under the direction of a former Yale University football player named Walter Camp, the game began to change radically in the early 1880s. Camp's changes to the game were so profound that he is still referred to as the "Father of American Football."

Camp devised a system of rules that gave the game a more organized look. His new rules included limiting teams to eleven players per side and establishing the line of scrimmage. He also devised a system of downs that required teams to advance the ball five yards within three plays to gain a first down (the modern-day system of four downs to make 10 yards became part of the game in 1912).

Though Walter Camp died about nine decades ago, his impact on the game of football is still recognized today. In football, he left behind a huge legacy—something he'll long be remembered for.

God has created and saved each of us who follow Him so that we can make an impact on the world around us, so that we can leave behind our own legacy. Yours may involve something as simple as being a good husband and father, or it may involve preaching the message of God's love to people who desperately need to hear it.

No matter what God has called you to do, keep in mind that He wants you to make an impact—and leave behind a lasting legacy.

"These commandments that I give you today are to be on your hearts. Impress them on your children. Talk about them when you sit at home and when you walk along the road, when you lie down and when you get up."
DEUTERONOMY 6:6–7

SCRIPTURE INDEX

CONTRIBUTORS

Joshua Cooley, a former fulltime sports writer/editor, is currently the children's minister at Chapel Hill Bible Church (North Carolina). He has written or contributed to seven other books. His latest solo project, *The One Year Devotions with Jesus* (Tyndale House), was published in 2015. His freelance work has been featured in a variety of publications, including *Sports Illustrated*, *FCA Magazine*, *Sports Spectrum*, *Thriving Family*, *Bethesda Magazine*, *Clubhouse* and *Highlights*. You can visit his website at www. joshuacooleyauthor.com. Pages 9, 12, 19, 21, 30, 39, 42, 51, 62, 68, 77, 88, 93, 103, 107, 117, 122, 132, 144, 189

Glenn A. Hascall is an accomplished writer with credits in more than one hundred books, including titles from Thomas Nelson, Bethany House, and Regal. His writing has appeared in numerous publications around the globe. He's also an award-winning broadcaster, lending his voice to animation and audio drama projects. Pages 10, 17, 25, 50, 56, 64, 74, 81, 94, 98, 100, 105, 110, 115, 123, 130, 135, 137, 141, 143, 147, 151, 152, 156, 162, 168, 171, 172, 178, 185

Paul Muckley is a long-time editor who has also written several books including *Know Your Bible*, *Bible Curiosities*, and *Playing with Purpose: Baseball Devotions*. He and his family live near Grand Rapids, Michigan. Pages 7, 14, 20, 27, 33, 40, 47, 53, 61, 69, 76, 82, 89, 96, 104, 112, 128, 150, 158, 167, 190

Allen M. Palmeri is a longtime Christian journalist who was first trained as a sportswriter. He has worked as a writer and an editor on newspaper and magazine staffs in four different states over the span of four decades. Allen is a graduate of Michigan State University who particularly enjoyed serving the Lord through two of the leading Christian sports magazines, *Sharing the VICTORY* and *Sports Spectrum*. Other stops on his media journey included: Battle Creek, Michigan; Biloxi, Mississippi; Cheyenne, Wyoming; and Jefferson City, Missouri. He and his wife, Susan, have four children and currently live in Jefferson City. Pages 8, 15, 16, 28, 31, 34, 43, 45, 48, 57, 58, 63, 65,

71, 78, 80, 87, 92, 97, 99, 108, 113, 120, 125, 126, 138, 142, 145, 146, 153, 157, 160, 169, 173, 175, 176, 179, 182, 188

Tracy M. Sumner is a freelance author, writer, and editor in Beaverton, Oregon. An avid outdoorsman, he enjoys fly-fishing on world-class Oregon waters. Pages 24, 26, 29, 32, 36, 37, 41, 44, 49, 52, 60, 67, 73, 75, 83, 90, 101, 109, 114, 121, 127, 133, 140, 149, 161, 166, 177, 183, 186, 191

Lee Warren is a freelance writer published in such varied venues as Discipleship Journal, Sports Spectrum, Crosswalk.com, and ChristianityToday.com. He is also the author of the book *Single Servings: 90 Devotions to Feed Your Soul*, and a regular sports columnist for a Christian newspaper. Lee makes his home in Omaha, Nebraska. Pages 11, 18, 23, 35, 46, 55, 66, 72, 79, 84, 95, 106, 111, 116, 119, 124, 129, 131, 136, 139, 154, 155, 159, 163, 165, 170, 174, 181, 184, 187

Russell Wight has served Jesus Christ as a Bible teacher since 1987 in over 300 churches through camps, kids clubs, and pulpits. He lives with his wife and three children on Cape Cod, Massachusetts. Pages 13, 59, 85, 91

ART CREDITS

Love Sports and the Outdoors?
Check Out. . .

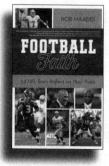

Football Faith by Rob Maaddi
Football Faith will inspire and encourage readers in their faith journey, as 52 NFL players share their stories and how they are chasing the success that only comes from being God's man and following His plan. Featuring personal stories from Russell Wilson, Aaron Rodgers, Colin Kaepernick, Deion Sanders, and dozens more—plus with a foreword from Coach Joe Gibbs.

Paperback / 978-1-63409-222-7 / $16.99

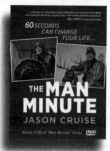

The Man Minute by Jason Cruise
Every "Man Minute" devotion is designed to be read in sixty seconds, yet a man will carry the insights he gleans into a lifelong journey of spiritual manhood. *The Man Minute* is packaged alongside a DVD featuring hunts—each couched in spiritual truths—with some of the most recognized hunters on the planet.

Hardback / 978-1-63058-718-5 / $16.99